softies

softies

Simple Instructions for 25 Plush Pals

therese laskey

FOREWORD BY LEAH KRAMER   PHOTOGRAPHS BY LAURIE FRANKEL

CHRONICLE BOOKS
SAN FRANCISCO

for Joan and Topsy

Text copyright © 2007 by **THERESE LASKEY**.
Foreword copyright © 2007 by **LEAH KRAMER**.
Photographs copyright © 2007 by **LAURIE FRANKEL**.
Illustrations copyright © 2007 by **KRISTEN RAY**.

Library of Congress Cataloging-in-Publication Data:

Laskey, Therese.

Softies : simple instructions for 25 plush pals / by Therese Laskey;
foreword by Leah Kramer; photographs by Laurie Frankel;
illustrations by Kristen Ray.

   p. cm.

 Includes index.
ISBN 978-0-8118-5652-2
1. Soft toy making. 2. Soft sculpture. I. Title.

TT174.3.L395 2007

745.592'4–dc22

                                  2006035543

Manufactured in China

Designed by **BROOKE JOHNSON**

Styling by **ETHEL BRENNAN**

The photographer would like to thank **SEAN DAGEN** for his amazing
photo assistance and **DAVID TUREK** of DT Productions for his fabulous
digital retouching.

10 9 8 7 6 5 4 3
Chronicle Books LLC
680 Second Street
San Francisco, California 94107

www.chroniclebooks.com

Shrinky Dinks is a registered trademark of K & B Innovations, Inc. Static
Guard is a registered trademark of Alberto-Culver Company.

contents

missing

Lucky Dog

foreword

One my earliest crafty memories from childhood is of my mother showing me how to sew a pillow. I thought that it was the most magical thing ever. I was enchanted by the fact that you could cut two matching pieces of fabric in any shape, hand sew them together inside out, turn the pieces right side out, and have a real live pillow. No matter how uneven your stitching was, it looked perfect. As a child, I found the idea that I could create such a thing with my own two hands to be so fulfilling and so empowering. For years I proceeded to make pillows in every conceivable shape and with every piece of fabric I could scrounge up (including secretly cutting up many things I wasn't supposed to, such as my sheets and curtains—thanks, Mom and Dad, for pretending not to notice!).

Looking at the projects in this book reminds me how a simple concept such as sewing fabric together and filling it with stuffing can be so satisfying. Even more important, it reminds me that this basic concept can be a "blank canvas" for creating objects with an enormous amount of originality, personality, and expression— whether they be cute, weird, edgy, or artful.

I love that there are so many different kinds of softies—big, little, skinny, round, misshapen, one eyed, three eyed, purple, green, striped—and that you can't help but love 'em all. Kind of a nice worldview, don't you think?

Softies are also one of those things that remind me why I love to craft and why I think crafting resonates so much right now. I believe that everyone has a creative voice inside and that crafting is such a limitless conduit for expression of this inner creativity. There are so many different kinds of crafts, and just when you think you've seen them all, a movement like softies comes along and provides you with a whole new road to explore.

I want to applaud Therese and the contributors to this book for finding a clever way for us to be grown-ups and still embrace the kid in each of us—by creating our own softies and displaying them proudly!

—Leah Kramer
founder of www.craftster.org
and author of *The Craftster Guide
to Nifty, Thrifty, and Kitschy Crafts*

introduction

Like most little girls, I grew up with a collection of stuffed animals—a few bears, a seal, a country mouse, and my favorite, a life-size pink poodle that matched my bubble gum–colored bedspread and walls. Back then, plush toys were cute and cuddly—and they were only animals. Now, thanks to a legion of independent crafters and artists, plush toys are no longer *just* cute, and no longer *just* animals. As you'll see in the projects that follow, a plush toy can also be an ice cream cone, a tooth, a friendly monster, or a tea bag. The cute bunnies and bears are here too, but look closely, because they're not always the ones you remember from childhood—some have scars, claws, or maybe an extra eye.

Called softies, these handmade plush toys are created for adults and are all the rage at indie craft fairs, art galleries, and online stores devoted to selling handmade goods.

Are softies a political statement about the value of handmade over that of mass-produced objects? Are they folk art? Or are they just a new way for us to use our sewing and embroidery skills? I think they're all those things, but, more important, softies are an outlet for creativity and imagination.

I first came across softies online at Loobylu (www.loobylu.com), a blog written by Claire Robertson of Australia. It may well have been one of the first to popularize softie making, through an online challenge called a Month of Softies (MOS). Each month features a theme, like "Under the Tree" for December or "April Showers" in the spring. Crafters make a softie and post a picture to the MOS group on www.flickr.com. It's not a competition, and no prizes are awarded. Rather, people participate for the pure joy of being creative and the fun of sharing one's work with an online community of like-minded individuals.

The wonderful softies created for a Month of Softies were the inspiration for this book. I hope *Softies* inspires you and others to have fun—and to make a softie.

the projects in the book

The softie projects were chosen for their originality and for the variety of styles and sewing techniques they represent. They also include a mix of easy projects for beginners and challenging ones for more experienced crafters. Some toys are machine sewn, a few are completely hand sewn, and others are made with a combination of both techniques. Most softies can be sewn entirely by hand—see "To Sew by Hand Instead of Machine" (page 12). Others are not sewn at all but made with other techniques like needle felting or crochet. (You'll find directions for needle felting in the projects themselves. Check your local yarn store for crochet classes.)

If you want to start with an easy softie, try the Paper Doll Dress (page 79) or the Scattered Flowers Pincushion (page 26). For a more challenging softie, Dorian the Dog (page 23) uses lots of different embroidery stitches but is still simple enough for a softie novice. Other softies are sure to make you smile—the Ice Cream Sandwich (page 83) has a funny face, and the Lonely Dollop (page 91) is a plush dollop of poo. For a sewing challenge, try Double Scoop (page 53) or Pig/Wolf (page 105).

the softie artists

Softie making is truly an international phenomenon. Twenty-five artist-crafters from the United States, Europe, Asia, Australia, and Israel contributed patterns for this book. All have been making things and crafting since childhood, and a few studied art or illustration in school. After each project you'll find a brief biography of the artist. Have fun making each softie, but remember that the designs belong to the artists who created them, and softies you make from their patterns cannot be sold.

When I asked artist Beck Wheeler why she makes toys, her reply struck me as representative of all the crafters showcased here: "Handmade is more than touching the fabric with my hands; it is touching something with my imagination, creating objects that radiate a uniqueness and embrace individuality."

Enjoy creating your own objects and expressing your imagination. And remember to have fun!

softies home ec

WHETHER YOU'RE A NOVICE CRAFTER or an experienced sewer looking for a new challenge, in this book you'll find a softie project that's right for you. But first you'll need to collect the right supplies. Below I've provided a list of some essential tools you'll need to get started. Some projects require more than the basics, so be sure to review the supplies list for any additional fabric, trim, or special items required for the project you choose.

Here are the basic supplies needed for all projects:

* embroidery needle
* hand-sewing needle
* fabric scissors
* dressmaker's chalk or erasable fabric-marking pen
* tape measure and ruler
* pencil
* straight pins
* card stock (optional, for making patterns)
* fiberfill

(Note: These are not repeated in the supplies list for each project.)

fabric, floss, and filler

FELT

Felt is a wonderful fabric for softie making. It comes in dozens of colors, is easy to work with (its edges won't fray), and is widely available in craft and fabric stores. There are three basic types of felt—acrylic craft felt, wool felt, and a wool-acrylic blend. Acrylic felt is generally sold in 9-by-12-inch sheets, and some retailers also sell it by the yard. Wool felt is harder to find in stores and is more expensive, but the fabric's "hand" (the way it feels) is so much nicer than that of craft felt. (See "Resources," page 118, for online sources.) Wool felt can be found in sheets of various sizes and is occasionally sold by the yard or even by the square inch. It also comes in a variety of weights—generally a medium-weight felt is best for softies. The wool-acrylic blend felt is a step up from craft felt and is less transparent than the 100 percent acrylic. Polar fleece is a good substitute for felt if you want a fuzzy texture for your softie.

WOOL ROVING

Two of the projects (Heartfelt Bunny on page 49 and Luella Bear and Her Baby Bear on page 61) are made with a technique called needle felting, which uses wool roving to make the softie. (Directions for needle felting are given in the project instructions.) Roving is sheep's wool fiber that has been cleaned and carded, or combed, and loosely twisted into a long roll or strand. Roving is sold in loosely folded "balls" or by the pound and is readily available from online stores that also carry felting needles (see "Resources," page 118).

FABRIC

Generally you will need less than ¼ yard of fabric to make a softie, so you can often use any leftover fabric scraps you have on hand. Printed cotton, linen, and corduroy are among the fabrics used to make the softies in this book. Vintage fabrics with cute patterns and interesting colors are also great for making or trimming softies. Look for vintage fabrics at thrift stores, garage sales, and flea markets, or recycle a vintage skirt and give it new life as a stuffed toy.

TRIM

Every softie has some form of embellishment—little bits of felt, special embroidery, beads, buttons, or ribbons. While you're out "thrifting" for fabric, look for trim too: lace, buttons, ribbons, and appliqués can all be cut off and used as decorations for your softie. Be open-minded about what qualifies as trim—plastic pieces from board games, doll hands, and items from the hardware store can personalize your softie.

EMBROIDERY FLOSS, THREAD, AND YARN

Floss comes in dozens of vibrant colors and finishes, including metallic, and is sold in craft and fabric stores as a 6-stranded thread wound in small skeins. When a project calls for 2 or 3 strands of floss, cut a piece of floss 12 to 18 inches long, and gently pull the strands apart by hand to get the number you need.

For machine sewn softies, use a thread color that matches the main fabric color. For hand sewn creations, use cotton embroidery floss as designated in the project instructions, or choose floss to match or contrast with the felt or fabric. Most of the softies in this book require either thread or floss for their construction or embellishment, but one project, Amigurumi Pink Bunny (page 75), is made with fingering or baby yarn, a very soft, lightweight type of yarn.

FILLER

Two basic types of filler are used to make the softies: fiberfill, a fluffy polyester stuffing, and weighted filler. Both are sold in craft stores and some fabric stores, and they come in generously sized bags that provide more than you'll need for one project. Fiberfill will get compressed inside the softie—on average, a handful of stuffing will be reduced to a third of its size—so you may end up using more filler to stuff your softie than you might expect. Alternative fillers include cotton batting, yarn, scraps of fabric, and even old pantyhose (be sure to cut off the elastic waistband before using).

Weighted filler (sometimes called plastic bean pellets) is used to help some softies balance and stand upright. Plastic pellets are easy to work with and do the job nicely, but if you prefer a "green" option, you might consider using lentils or rice. However, in a humid climate, the lentils or rice may absorb moisture and clump or get moldy, ruining the shape of your softie. And a softie filled with a food product could attract mice or bugs. But, that being said, I use lentils and live in a humid climate, and I haven't had any problems with this filler.

Most softies look best when they are chock-full of stuffing—it gives them a fuller, more finished look. Follow the project directions to produce the same look as the softie pictured, or adjust the amount of stuffing to fit your own style. Once you've fully stuffed your softie, follow the directions in the project for sewing the opening closed. Below are some general tips for getting good results with stuffing:

* Using your fingers, stuff the softie with small amounts of filler, adding a little bit at a time. Don't try to jam in one big glob of filler; it won't save time and it may look lumpy.

* Be sure to work the stuffing into all the edges and corners of the softie.

* If you find it hard to reach tiny areas with your fingers, try using a crochet hook, a chopstick, or any long, narrow household item—even an unsharpened pencil—to push the stuffing into the tight spots.

* Be especially careful to stuff the softie's arms and legs fully so that they are firm and stand out from the body.

* Make sure the stuffing is even throughout.

* When you think you've stuffed enough, add a little more!

softie sewing techniques

Sewing softies is easy! The sewing techniques are not complicated and are easy to pick up if you're new to the task. Some of the softies are sewn by machine, while others are sewn by hand, and still others are constructed using a combination of machine and hand sewing. If you don't own a machine, don't despair—every project in the book can be sewn entirely by hand (see "To Sew by Hand Instead of Machine," page 12). Whether you're sewing by machine or hand, there are just a few basics to keep in mind and a few terms you'll need to be familiar with. You'll find them all explained in the following pages.

PATTERNS

In the envelope bound at the back of this book, you'll find sheets with patterns for the softies. To work with these patterns, cut out the pattern pieces from the sheet, pin the pieces on the fabric designated in the project's instructions, and cut carefully around the pinned patterns. Alternatively, you may want to retrace and cut these pattern pieces from card stock (a heavyweight paper) in order to trace the pattern outline directly on the fabric. To trace the pattern, use dressmaker's chalk or an erasable fabric-marking pen. Then just cut along the traced lines.

Note that, for patterns that involve machine sewing, the pattern pieces already include a ¼-inch seam allowance unless otherwise noted in the project instructions (see "Seam Allowances" for more information on stitching seams). Pattern pieces for softies to be sewn by hand have no seam allowance, since the pieces will be simply sewn together at the cut edges.

Some patterns contain placement marks, indicating, for example, where arms or legs should join a body or when a pattern edge should be cut on the fold of the fabric. If you're an experienced sewer, you'll notice that some of the markings that you would ordinarily find on garment patterns do not appear on these pattern pieces. This is because softies are much more forgiving than garments, so it's not crucial to position the eyes on the face or trim on the body exactly where they are on the original. To position facial features or trim, either look at the photograph of the softie you're making to see approximately where to place them, or customize the toy by adjusting those positions as you like.

When you do find placement marks on a pattern, you'll need to transfer those marks to the cut fabric pieces with dressmaker's chalk or an erasable fabric-marking pen *before* unpinning the pattern piece. If you're machine sewing the softie with right sides together, you'll transfer the marks onto the wrong side of the fabric. If you're hand sewing the softie with wrong sides together, you'll transfer the mark lightly onto the right side of the fabric.

For projects made with pieces that are a standard shape, such as a circle, square, or rectangle, you'll find cutting dimensions provided in the project instructions. You can either mark the dimensions directly on the fabric, or draw the shapes on card stock and then cut them out for use as your pattern. For a circle, either draw the shape

freehand, or trace a round object like a glass and then measure and trim the circle to the diameter given in the instructions. For an oval, draw the shape freehand, or draw a rectangle using the dimensions given and then round the corners with your scissors. Whether you're marking directly on your fabric or making patterns from card stock, be sure to double-check the pattern dimensions *before* cutting. Since these pieces sometimes need to be joined with other pieces, accuracy is important.

RIGHT VERSUS WRONG SIDE OF THE FABRIC

Many woven fabrics, like printed cotton for example, have distinctly different "right" and "wrong" sides. Accordingly, you'll find the terms *right side* and *wrong side* used throughout the sewing directions. The *right side* of the fabric is the front, or face, of the fabric—that is, the side that you want to show on the outside of your softie. The *wrong side* of the fabric will be turned to the inside of the softie and will not show on the finished piece. But keep in mind that, unlike woven fabric, felt has no right or wrong side—both sides are the same.

Most of the instructions for sewing softies by machine will direct you to position the two cut pieces of fabric with *right sides facing* (and with the edges aligned). This means that you will be sewing the seam on the wrong side of the two aligned pieces. After sewing the seam, you will turn the softie *right side out,* and in doing so you will hide the stitches of the seam you just sewed and keep the seam allowances on the inside of the softie.

Occasionally (for example, in Tramp Heart Bear on page 45), project directions call for machine sewing the two cut pieces with *wrong sides together.* As a result, you don't need to turn the softie right side out after you've finished sewing—you're already working on it right side out. The seam and the seam allowance will, by the designer's intent, show on the finished softie. Because Tramp Heart Bear is made of felt, however, the seam allowances' cut edges, which show on the right side, won't unravel or fray.

SEAM ALLOWANCES

Unless otherwise noted in the project instructions, all the seams on machine sewn pieces should be sewn with a ¼-inch seam allowance.

As explained earlier (see "Patterns"), this seam allowance is already built in to the provided patterns for machine sewn softies. However, the stitching line for this ¼-inch seam is not marked on the patterns. Therefore, you'll need to use the ¼-inch stitching-guide mark on the base plate of your sewing machine to position the aligned cut edges of the fabric so that they are ¼ inch from the needle. If your base plate doesn't have stitching-guide marks, mark the plate by positioning a small Post-it Note (or a rubber band slipped over the free arm of the machine) ¼ inch to the right of the needle; this will serve as your stitching guide.

Instructions for most garment and home-decorating sewing projects direct you to press the seam allowances open or to one side after sewing a seam. In the case of machine sewn softies, there's no need to worry about pressing the seam allowances before turning the project right side out. Stuffing the softie with filler will do the job of flattening the seam allowances on the inside for you. (And, of course, in the case of softies sewn by hand, there are no seam allowances to worry about.)

TOPSTITCHING VERSUS EDGE STITCHING

While most seams in these projects are sewn with a ¼-inch seam allowance, occasionally the directions call for topstitching or edge stitching. *Topstitching* refers to stitching on the fabric's right side more than ⅛ inch from an edge; it can be used to add decorative stitching, join two pieces of fabric, or do both at once. For example, in the case of Treeling (page 37), the directions call for topstitching down the center of the leaves in the treetop with contrasting thread, which both decorates and attaches the leaves.

Edge stitching refers to stitching very close to an edge (usually ⅛ inch or less from the edge) and, like topstitching, can be used to decorate, reinforce, or attach the fabric. In the case of Pig/Wolf (page 105), the wolf teeth are edge stitched over the gums.

GATHERING STITCHES

Occasionally project directions call for gathering a length of fabric. You can gather fabric with either machine stitches or hand stitches. To gather by machine, loosen the tension setting on the bobbin thread (check your machine manual for information on how to adjust the tension setting) so that the thread in the stitches on the back of the fabric will be looser than that in the stitches on the front, and leave thread tails a couple of inches long at the beginning and end of the line of gathering stitches. After taking the fabric out of the machine, gently pull the thread tail on the bobbin thread (the one on the back of the fabric) at each end of your stitching line to draw up, or gather, the fabric. Spread the gathers out evenly over the line of stitches, and secure the gathers at each end of the stitching line with a knot or a stitch or two (thread the tails into a needle to hand sew these final securing stitches).

To sew a line of gathering stitches by hand, use a running stitch. At the end of the stitching line, do not knot the thread; rather, leave a several-inch-long thread tail. Gently pull the thread tail to gather up the stitches, and evenly distribute the resulting puckers over the length of the line of stitches. When you've adjusted the gathers to the length you need, secure the gathers by taking a couple of stitches in place at the end of the stitching line and knotting the thread on the back of the fabric. Clip off any excess thread.

DEALING WITH CURVES

Almost every softie project has a rounded curve somewhere—an arm on a bear or the face of a dog, for example—and it's helpful to know a couple of basic sewing techniques to use on curves to help make them lie flat and produce nice, finished edges when the project is turned right side out. Unattended curves may make the fabric bunch up inside the softie, or they may cause the fabric to pull too tightly, making it hard to turn the softie right side out. As a result, you may find it difficult to get smooth, finished edges. There are two basic kinds of curves—inner curves and outer curves—and there are two techniques for handling them, clipping and notching.

If an inner curve is sharp rather than gentle, it may have too much fabric in it to allow the fabric to lie flat in the small, curved space. Clipping the fabric enables it to fold over itself and lie flat on the inside of the project. To clip a curved seam, use your scissors to make small cuts into both seam allowances around the curve, as shown in the illustration. When you're clipping, be very careful not to cut into the stitched seam itself.

If an outer curve is sharp, the fabric needed to stretch around the curve will pull a bit, and the seam will not lie flat on the inside of the softie. Notching the seam allowances on an outer curve enables fabric to stretch comfortably around the curve and allows the seam to lie flat. To notch an outer curve, follow the illustration and cut tiny triangles out of the seam allowances. Again, be careful not to cut into the seam's stitches when you're notching.

If you're unsure whether you have an inner or outer curve, don't worry. The project directions will tell you whether to clip or notch the seam allowances. And once you use these techniques a few times, you'll begin to see when your fabric needs room to spread (and therefore needs to be notched) and when there's too much of it (and it needs to be clipped).

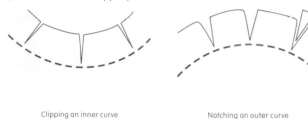

Clipping an inner curve   Notching an outer curve

TO SEW BY HAND INSTEAD OF MACHINE

If you don't own a sewing machine and want to sew a softie by hand (even if the directions call for machine sewing), it's easy to do. Follow the project directions exactly as they're written, keeping the fabric's right sides facing for sewing. When the instructions tell you to sew a seam by machine, sew a small, tight, even running stitch or backstitch by hand instead.

A second way to convert a machine sewn project to a hand sewn one involves making a few changes in the directions, as outlined as follows. Be aware, though, that the resulting softie will not look exactly like the one shown in the book: the seam allowances will show on the outside of the finished softie. This is not necessarily a bad thing, since hand sewing gives the softie a charming, crafted look. The technique works fine on softies without sharp curves but is less successful on a project like The Lookout (page 29), whose sharply curved tail would lose its definition since the seam allowances would bunch up in the curve.

To convert softie instructions for hand rather than machine sewing, follow the steps below:

step 1. sew with wrong sides of the fabric together

When joining two cut pieces together by sewing, place the wrong sides of fabric together. Because this places the seam allowances on the outside of the softie, it's probably a good idea to substitute felt if the project instructions call for a different fabric, since the edges on felt won't fray.

step 2. pick an embroidery stitch to replace the machine stitching

Any one of several embroidery stitches will close a seam—backstitch, running stitch, blanket stitch, and whipstitch (see "Hand Embroidery Stitches," on the facing page)—so picking one is really a matter of personal choice and design preference. Keep your stitches nice and even, without a lot of space between them, so the softie is closed securely and the stuffing stays put.

step 3. use care when selecting a floss color, since your stitches will show

Using floss in a color that contrasts with the color of the fabric will give the work a nice, handmade look. For a subtler style, match the floss color to the fabric.

step 4. consider an optional finish for edges

Since your seam allowances will show on the right side, you may want to finish the edges by cutting them with pinking shears or decorative-edge scissors. To do this, you'll need a little more room on the edge than the ¼-inch seam allowance built into the pattern, so make sure to cut all the pattern pieces ¼ inch bigger all around. When pinking or using decorative-edge scissors to cut the edges, be careful to not cut too close to your stitches and accidentally open the seam. Also, if you decide to use decorative-edge scissors, look for scissors made for fabric, not for paper and scrapbooking.

HAND EMBROIDERY STITCHES

Hand embroidery is fun to do and adds a distinctive, handmade look to your softie. There are seven basic hand embroidery stitches used to make the softies: backstitch, blanket stitch, French knot, lazy daisy stitch, running stitch, satin stitch, and whipstitch. The project directions will specify the stitches used, but sometimes you can substitute other stitches to get a different look. For instance, to close a seam, regardless of the stitch called for in the pattern, you could use a whipstitch, backstitch, blanket stitch, or running stitch. You could also substitute embroidery stitches for the decorative beads, buttons, or other trim called for in a pattern. Or, if you want to keep embroidery to a minimum, you can sometimes glue on certain elements, like the eyes onto a softie face, instead of embroidering them. The key here is to experiment and use your imagination to customize the project.

Here are a few tips for successful embroidery. Always keep your stitches and the space between them the same length. Be consistent with your sewing tension (in other words, how tight or loose you make your stitches). If you're new to embroidery, you may want to practice the stitches on a scrap of fabric before beginning the softie.

Backstitch

The backstitch is one of the most basic embroidery stitches and is used decoratively in many of the softie projects (see the nice backstitched mouth on Lucky Dog, page 33). A backstitch gets its name because you create it by moving the needle a stitch backward before moving it forward to create the next stitch.

Here's how to make this stitch: The backstitch is worked from right to left. Place your threaded needle under the fabric and bring it up all the way through at the point where you want to begin (point 1 in illustration A). Insert the needle into point 2, go under the fabric, and come back out at point 3, which is one stitch length ahead of point 1. You now have one completed stitch.

To make the next stitch, insert the needle into point 2 in illustration B (this was originally point 1 in illustration A), and repeat the sequence, keeping your stitches the same length and tension, and moving backward and forward in a straight line. If you keep the stitches small and close, they will closely resemble stitches made by a sewing machine, as shown in illustration C.

A   B   C

Blanket Stitch

The blanket stitch is typically used to close seams or add decoration when layering elements. Paper Doll Dress (page 79), uses a blanket stitch to close seams.

Here's how to make this stitch: The blanket stitch is generally worked from left to right, with the thread moving between two parallel lines. Bring the threaded needle up through the fabric at point 1 in illustration A, on the bottom line. Then insert it at point 2 on the top line, and come back out at point 3, directly below. Before pulling the needle all the way through, make sure the thread is under the needle, as shown in illustration A.

Start the next stitch by inserting the needle at point 2 in illustration B, and bring the needle out at point 3, as shown. Continue working the stitches across the fabric this way, keeping their height and width the same, as shown in illustration C.

A   B   C

French Knot

The French knot is easy to make and produces a nice, rounded knot that can be used for the center of a flower or the eyes on your softie. You could also add French knots to create a series of decorative dots on the softie.

Here's how to make this stitch: Start the knot by bringing the needle up at point 1 in illustration A. Hold the thread tightly in your left hand (or in your right hand if you're a left-handed sewer), and wrap it around the needle twice, as shown in illustration B. Carefully insert the needle *near* point 1, and pull the thread through as shown in illustration C. (Be careful not to use the same exact hole, or the thread will pull through and you'll have to start all over.) That's it—you've made a French knot. To make a bigger knot, wrap more twists of yarn around the needle and/or use more strands of floss in your needle.

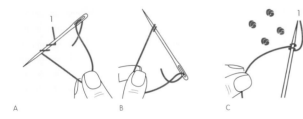

A   B   C

Lazy Daisy Stitch

The lazy daisy stitch is a variation of the classic chain stitch and is designed to look like the petals on a flower. This stitch is used on only one project in this book, Dorian the Dog (page 23), but you could add it as a personal decorative touch to other softies. Floral shapes are welcome additions to most projects!

Here's how to make this stitch: The lazy daisy stitch is worked in a circle. Bring the needle out from below at point 1 in illustration A, insert the needle back through the same hole, and exit at point 2—all in one smooth movement. Keep the thread under the needle as you pull it through. Then insert the needle at point 3 in illustration B

over the loop and bring the needle out at new point 1. Continue stitching around a center point to form a circle of petals, as shown in illustration C.

A   B   C

Running Stitch

The running stitch is simple to make. Just be careful to keep the length of your stitches and the space between them the same length. The Wee Robot (page 111) is a good example of how a running stitch is used to decorate a curved edge.

Here's how to make this stitch: The running stitch is generally sewn from right to left. Bring your threaded needle up at point 1 in illustration A, and back down through the fabric at point 2. Skip a space that is equal to the length of the stitch you've just made and come up at point 3. Repeat to continue the line.

A

Satin Stitch

Satin stitches are used to fill in an area with floss. They make very nice noses on softies—see Snow Bunny (page 19). The stitch itself is easy to do, but it may take some practice to get the fill stitches lined up evenly and flat. Be sure to fill in the designated area with enough stitches so that the fabric underneath doesn't show through.

Here's how to make this stitch: Bring a threaded needle up through the fabric at point 1 in illustration A, and then insert it back down in the fabric at point 2. Bring the needle back up at point 3, next to point 1, and repeat the process (as shown in illustrations B and C) to fill in the area. For a round satin-stitch nose, it's best to start the first stitch in the middle of the nose and then fill in to the right and left with successively smaller stitches. Be consistent so that both filled sides match and the nose is round.

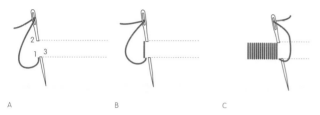

A   B   C

Whipstitch

A whipstitch is a good stitch for closing a seam—and it's very forgiving for a beginning embroiderer since it's intended to have an unfinished sort of look. Party Cake (page 67) uses this stitch for all of its seams. Using a contrasting color of floss with your whipstitch will make it stand out, as it does on the base of Lonely Dollop (page 91). The length of the stitch and angle may vary depending on the design and size of the softie.

Here's how to make this stitch: Working with two cut edges held together with wrong sides facing, bring the needle up at point 1, then insert the needle from behind fabric and bring it up at point 2. Continue taking angled stitches across the seam, keeping the angle, stitch length, and distance between them even.

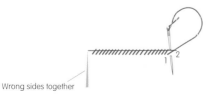

Wrong sides together

creating original softie designs

Once you've made a few softies, you many want to start creating your own designs and patterns. If you are drawing challenged, as I am, think about using common objects, like a glass for a circle, to create an outline for a pattern. Or look for images that you can trace to make a pattern and use to cut out a softie. A little sparrow outline is easy, for example. You could sew several in different colors of felt with unique trim and bead eyes, and fashion them into a mobile. Images of birds and other things are everywhere—in books, in magazines, on wallpaper, and even on plates. Other sources of images to trace are coloring books, scrapbooking stencils, and die-cut greeting cards.

Keep the following in mind as you develop your designs:

* Use these projects to experiment with techniques and stitches.
* Softie making is not like a spelling bee—perfection is *not* a requirement. The charm of softies is their handmade, unique quality.
* Ribbons, rickrack, buttons, and beads are fun embellishments that can add to, or even inspire, a design.
* Felt is forgiving and easy to work with.
* A softie can be anything—a house, an imaginary animal, fabulous food, an internal organ. There are no limits.

projects

snow bunny

DIFFICULTY LEVEL : easy　　**FINISHED SIZE** : **LARGE BUNNY** 5¾ inches wide by 12¼ inches high　　**SEW** : by machine and hand
MEDIUM BUNNY 4¼ inches wide by 9¾ inches high
SMALL BUNNY 4 inches wide by 9 inches high

This bunny is a perfect project for a beginner. The basic elements are simple to sew, and you can embellish it with different trims to make it unique. The body is made with already embroidered linen, but plain fabric or felt would also work well. The ears are made with a pashmina-like fabric, whose soft texture contrasts nicely with the rougher linen. The pom-pom tail, an essential finishing touch, helps the bunny balance and stand upright.

embroidery stitches

blanket stitch

whipstitch

satin stitch

materials

FABRIC: ¼ yard off-white or natural shade of embroidered linen for the body; 7¼-by-3¾-inch scrap of pashmina, felt, or flannel for ears and bottom panel

FLOSS: white for the ears; light brown for eyes; red for the nose

YARN: any bulky yarn for pompom tail, about 23 yards, in off-white, natural, tan, or a blend of two colors

TRIM: beads; floss; bells; buttons; lace, ribbons

OTHER: weighted filler

Note: See page 8 for the list of basic supplies needed for all projects.

cut from patterns

FROM EMBROIDERED LINEN
2 bodies

FROM PASHMINA, FELT, OR FLANNEL
2 ears

cut freehand

FROM PASHMINA, FELT, OR FLANNEL
1 bottom panel circle (2¾ inches in diameter)

continued

19

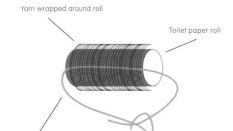

tips

* Play with the size of the ears by making them longer for a floppier look.

* Embroider the ears, adding a lazy daisy stitch or a series of French knots down the center and a running stitch around the edges.

* Experiment with plaid flannels and flower prints for the body or ears for a different look.

Yarn wrapped around roll

Toilet paper roll

Separate piece of yarn slipped under wrapped yarn and tied loosely

Remove yarn from roll, and tightly tie knot of securing yarn. Then cut yarn wraps, and trim to complete pom-pom.

sew

Note: The directions and pattern provided are to make the medium bunny.

step 1. make the body

a. With **right** sides facing and raw edges aligned, machine stitch the body pieces with a ¼-inch seam allowance, leaving the straight bottom edge open. Turn the body **right** side out.

b. Place the bottom panel over the right side of the body opening, aligning the panel's widest part with the body's side seams, and sew it halfway around the body by hand, using a blanket stitch. You'll use the opening to insert stuffing and weighted filler in the body.

c. Stuff the body tightly with fiberfill, leaving the bottom inch or so empty. Then fill the empty space with weighted filler, which will help the bunny stand upright.

d. Finish sewing the bottom panel closed by hand.

step 2. make the ears

a. Fold the fabric for one ear in half lengthwise, with **wrong** sides together and the edges aligned. Sew the edges together by hand with a whipstitch, leaving the bottom open.

b. Fill the ear generously with fiberfill, and sew the bottom opening closed with a whipstitch.

c. Repeat steps 2a and 2b to make the second ear.

d. Sew the ears to the top of the bunny's head, using a whipstitch.

step 3. make the pom-pom tail

a. Take a cardboard cylinder from a roll of toilet paper, and wind yarn around it, as shown in the diagram at left, until covered from end to end. The more yarn you wind, the bigger the pom-pom will be. (We wound the yarn 180 times to get our pom-pom.)

b. Cut a separate 12-inch piece of yarn, and slip it underneath the wound strands of yarn on the toilet paper roll. (If you find that the yarn tends to break easily, use string instead to tie off the yarn.) Slip the yarn off the cardboard, tie the ends of the 12-inch piece of yarn together tightly, and make a knot.

c. Cut the loops of the yarn, and trim the yarn ends to make a nice, round pom-pom.

d. Sew the pom-pom to the body by hand, taking 5 or 6 stitches in place and making sure to stitch through to the middle of the pom-pom to secure it properly.

step 4. embellish the bunny

a. Use small silver beads for eyes, placing them fairly far apart and attaching them with floss or thread. Make 4 to 6 long, straight stitches, and catch the bead for the eye with one or more stitches. This will help define the eyes.

b. Embroider a nose using a satin stitch.

c. Embellish your bunny with beads, floss, bells, buttons, lace, ribbons, fabric cutouts, and other items.

ARTIST BIO

Tamar Mogendorff
www.tmogy.com

- - - - - - - - - -

Grew up: On a kibbutz in Israel

Creative influences: Her German grandmother and Dutch father influence her art. As a child, Tamar made softie snails, bears, and dolls as gifts for her playmates on the kibbutz.

Why she makes what she makes: Inspired by her dreams of sparkling, magical worlds, Tamar makes bunnies, swans, geese, deer heads, snow owls, and sea horses. "Sometimes when I shop for fabric, I 'see' the kind of creature it will become."

dorian the dog

DIFFICULTY LEVEL : moderate   **FINISHED SIZE** : 3 inches wide by 3½ inches high   **SEW** : by hand

Dorian the Dog is as light as a feather, so he's perfect for hanging as an ornament! And you can have fun embellishing him with different embroidery stitches. The imaginative flower overlay is a great technique that could be used with other projects in the book. Or try other design elements, like hearts, stars, crosses, circles, or leaves, in place of the flowers.

embroidery stitches

blanket stitch

French knot

lazy daisy stitch

whipstitch

satin stitch

Note: When sewing with floss, use 6 strands unless otherwise noted.

materials

FELT: 1 sheet of white for the body; scraps of blue, pink, yellow and brown for the eyes, flowers, tail, and ears

FLOSS: orange; burgundy; light blue; teal; moss green; rose pink; turquoise; light pink; red; aqua; tan; white; brown

OTHER: fabric glue

Note: See page 8 for the list of basic supplies needed for all projects.

cut from patterns

FROM FELT

2 white bodies

1 pink tulip flower

1 yellow diamond flower

2 brown tails

2 brown ears

cut freehand

FROM FELT

2 blue eye circles, ⅜ inch in diameter

continued

tips

- To hang Dorian as an ornament, add a narrow ribbon at the top of the head as you're stitching around the body.

- This project uses 13 different colors of floss, but create your own color scheme and reduce the number of colors if you like.

- Use glue sparingly—just enough to attach the pieces. Always stitch over the glue after it has dried, in order to secure the element properly.

sew

step 1. embroider the eyes and flowers

a. Lightly glue an eye on the face of each half of the body.

b. Using a single strand of orange floss, embroider a blanket stitch around each eye. Then, using 6 strands of burgundy floss, make a French knot in the center of the eye, and using 6 strands of light blue floss, sew 3 French knots underneath it.

c. Lightly glue both flowers to the lower front side of the body.

d. Working with teal and moss green floss, embroider a stem for the tulip using a straight stitch, and make leaves using a lazy daisy stitch.

e. With a single strand of rose pink floss, embroider a blanket stitch around the pink tulip.

f. For the diamond flower, use turquoise floss to make small whipstitches around flower.

g. Switching to 6 strands of light pink floss, stitch a straight stitch across the diamond flower in both directions and then add a red cross stitch in the center of the flower using a single strand of red floss.

h. Make a stem for this flower by sewing a straight stitch using 6 strands of turquoise floss.

i. With 6 strands of aqua floss, embroider a lazy daisy leaf.

step 2. make the tail

a. Align and stitch both pieces of the tail together, using a single strand of tan floss and a blanket stitch; leave a small opening at the straight edge of the tail. Fill the tail with fiberfill, and stitch it closed.

b. Insert the base of the tail in between the two body pieces placed **wrong** sides together. Stitch the tail securely to the inside of one side of the dog body.

step 3. make the body

a. Align and stitch the two parts of the body together with a single strand of white floss and a blanket stitch.

step 4. add the ears

a. Lightly glue an ear on each side of the body. Add a single-strand stitch or two of tan floss at the top of each ear to securely attach it to the body.

step 5. embroider a nose

a. Using 6 strands of brown floss, embroider a satin stitch nose.

ARTIST BIO

Chika Mori

CHIKAGRAPHY
www.chikagraphy.com

Grew up: Japan, and Rome, Italy

Creative influences: Her great-grandmother, grandmother, and mother all made crafty things. Chika started sketching imaginary creatures and writing stories about their lives as a child. The drawings became patterns, and she sewed her first felt duck with a white body, beady eyes, and a big yellow beak when she was nine years old.

Why she makes what she makes: "I'm inspired by many things," she says. "Nature, old children's books, Scandinavian designs from the '40s to '60s, Bakelite buttons, old kitchenware, but mostly by the Japanese, sawdust-stuffed animals from the '50s and '60s. I just love old stuff."

scattered flowers pincushion

A pincushion is a sweet gift for anyone girly or crafty. Follow the directions, or adjust the designs by covering the top (and sides) with anything you can imagine: stars, hearts, pearl beads, rick-rack, sequins, one big flower, or any little trinket you find at the flea market. A pincushion can be easily customized for holidays and birthdays, too.

embroidery stitches

French knot

blanket stitch

Note: When sewing with floss, use 2 strands unless otherwise noted.

materials

FELT: scraps of light pink for flowers; 1 sheet of hot pink for pincushion

FLOSS: light pink

OTHER: weighted filler

Note: See page 8 for the list of basic supplies needed for all projects.

cut from pattern

FROM FELT

24 light pink flower shapes

cut freehand

FROM FELT

2 hot pink pieces (top and bottom), each 3 inches square

1 hot pink side band, 1⅜ by 12 inches

continued

tips

* You may want to make a paper funnel to add more filler as you're closing up the pincushion.

* For an aromatic pincushion, try adding dried lavender buds to the filler.

ARTIST BIO

Cassi Griffin

BELLA DIA
www.belladia.typepad.com

- - - - - - - - - - - -

Grew up: Western half of the United States

Creative influences: Cassi's grandmothers, her mother, and an aunt were all creative and taught her to embroider, crochet, tat, and make tin flowers and bath salts.

Why she makes what she makes: She made her first pincushion simply because she needed one! With more than one hundred different pincushion designs, Cassi seems to have limitless creativity with this form.

sew

step 1. embellish the pincushion top

a. Stack two flower pieces, offset slightly so that they're not perfectly aligned, and attach the pair to the pincushion top piece with 3 to 5 French knots using 3 strands of floss for each knot. Continue stacking and attaching pairs of flowers, creating a random, scattered look by placing a few flowers close to the edge so that they seem to be about to fall off.

step 2. mark and attach the side band to the pincushion top

a. Starting on one long side of the side band, measure and mark with a pin every 3 inches; these marked points will become the side band's corners. Attach the side band to the top of the pincushion by matching up a corner of the top with a corner of the side band, and pin each corner and the side band in between the corners in place. Stitch the top and side band together using a blanket stitch. Be careful to keep your tension even as you sew around the corners, or you may run short of fabric. Or simply cut the side band piece a little longer, and trim it when you get to the end.

b. Stitch the top ends of the side band together at the fourth corner, trimming any overlap or tucking it under before joining the two ends.

step 3. attach the side band to the pincushion bottom

a. Sew the bottom piece of the pincushion to the side band using a blanket stitch, leaving one side of the square open.

step 4. stuff the pincushion

a. Stuff the top three-quarters of the pincushion with fiberfill.

b. Add weighted filler to fill in the remaining space in the pincushion.

step 5. finish the pincushion

a. Sew the last side of the square closed, using a blanket stitch.

b. Manipulate the finished pincushion with your hands, shifting the stuffing as needed to make a nice square shape.

the lookout

DIFFICULTY LEVEL : easy   **FINISHED SIZE** : **WHALE** 10 inches wide by 7 inches high   **SEW** : by machine and hand
BIRD 2 inches high

Sometimes the smallest detail catches your eye. With this softie, the blue rickrack ocean is a great touch. There are lots of other interesting materials here: the feather on the bird's head, the foam for his beak, and the googly eyes on both the bird and the whale. This softie design is quick to sew, and you get to use a hot-glue gun.

embroidery stitches

running stitch

whipstitch

 Note: When sewing with floss, use 6 strands unless otherwise noted.

materials

FELT: 2 sheets of gray for whale; scrap of purple (3 by 4 inches) for bird

FLOSS: black; ivory; navy

THREAD: gray; purple

TRIM: 10½ inches blue chenille rickrack, ⅝ inch wide; 1 small red feather; scraps of yellow and red foam sheets, 2 mm thick; 1 googly eye for the bird, 5 mm, or approximately ⅛ inch in diameter; 1 googly eye for the whale, 15 mm, or approximately ½ inch in diameter

OTHER: hot-glue gun, superglue

Note: See page 8 for the list of basic supplies needed for all projects.

cut from patterns

FROM FELT

2 gray whale bodies

2 purple bird bodies

cut freehand

FROM FOAM SHEET

1 yellow bird beak

2 yellow bird feet

1 red bird collar

continued

sew

step 1. sew the whale body

a. On one whale body, embroider a mouth with running stitches in black floss: start 1½ inches above the bottom edge on the left side, curve the stitches slightly upward to about 2¼ inches from the bottom edge at the mouth's center, and end the stitches 2 inches from the bottom edge and about 2 inches from the right side. Make each stitch approximately ¼ inch in length, and keep them evenly spaced.

b. Using ivory floss, sew a single, long straight stitch from the center of each mouth stitch to the bottom edge of the body.

c. Machine stitch the body pieces with **right** sides together, leaving a 5-inch opening on the bottom edge for stuffing. Turn the body **right** side out.

d. Stuff the body tightly with fiberfill.

e. Using thread, hand sew the opening closed with a whipstitch, and then whipstitch around the whale body with navy floss for a decorative look.

step 2. add the ocean

a. Take the rickrack, fold each end under about ¾ inch; hot glue the folded edges in place. This will finish the edges and make the piece sturdy.

b. Hot glue the rickrack to the bottom of the whale.

step 3. make the bird

a. Machine stitch the two halves of the bird's body with **right** sides together, leaving the bottom open.

b. Stuff the bird with fiberfill, and sew the opening closed by hand, using thread and a small whipstitch.

continued

ARTIST BIO

Michelle Valigura

THE GIRLS PRODUCTIONS
www.thegirlsproductions.com

- - - - - - - - - - - - -

Grew up: Pacific Northwest

Creative influences: Michelle loves to figure out how to make things and has pursued that passion as a movie theater projectionist, hand painter of designer shoes, and Rose Parade float maker.

Why she makes what she makes: When she heard about a plush-toy art show, she jumped at the chance to participate. She quickly figured out how to make a softie and created her first toys just two weeks before the show opened.

c. Add a tiny bit of superglue to the feather's stem, and insert it in the top seam of the bird's head by poking the stem between two stitches.

d. Sew the base of the feather to the bird body with a few stitches to secure it.

e. Hot glue the foam beak, feet, and collar to the bird. Use a toothpick for more control when applying the glue.

step **4. finish the whale and bird**

a. Hot glue the bird to the top of the whale.

b. Use superglue to attach the googly eyes to the bird and whale.

lucky dog

DIFFICULTY LEVEL : moderate   **FINISHED SIZE** : 5 inches wide by 10 inches high   **SEW** : by machine and hand

A fast and easy project, this little guy is made with terry cloth, which gives him a cozy appearance that looks great with the felt face and ears. Terry cloth frays, so it's best sewn with a machine. If you want to hand sew your Lucky Dog, use felt.

embroidery stitches

running stitch

backstitch

blanket stitch

Note: When sewing with floss, use 2 strands unless otherwise noted.

materials

FABRIC: ¼ yard tan terry cloth for the body

FELT: scraps of brown, white, black, and red for the face, eyes, nose, ears, and collar

FLOSS: white; black; brown

TRIM: 1 button, ⅝ inch in diameter

OTHER: weighted filler; Shrinky Dinks plastic or white felt for the name tag; a narrow ribbon to hang the tag from (optional, see tip)

Note: See page 8 for the list of basic supplies needed for all projects.

cut from patterns

FROM TERRY CLOTH
2 tan bodies

FROM FELT
2 brown ears

cut freehand

FROM FELT
2 white eye circles, ¾ inch in diameter

2 black eye circles, ½ inch in diameter

1 black rounded nose triangle, ¾ inch in diameter

1 brown oval face, 3 inches in diameter

1 red collar, ⅝ by 8½ inches

FROM SHRINKY DINKS PLASTIC OR FELT
1 name tag, 1 inch in diameter (optional, see tip)

continued

33

ARTIST BIO

Leesa J. Perry

LITTLE MUNKI
www.littlemunki.squarespace.com

Grew up: Brisbane, Australia

Creative influences: As a child, Leesa longed for a handmade rag doll of her own and tried to "will" one off the pages of a craft book. Later, in college, Leesa fell in love with the excesses of the baroque and rococo design movements, as well as the atmospheric photographs by Julia Margaret Cameron.

Why she makes what she makes: The mother of a small child, Leesa makes softies that will please her little boy, and she often begins with the facial expressions of the TV cartoon characters he loves. Leesa likes to keep her designs simple to sew and fast to make.

sew

step 1. assemble the felt face

a. Refer to the photo for the eye and nose positions, and sew them on the oval face with running stitches near their cut edges, and use floss in a color that matches the felt pieces you're sewing. Stitch the whites of the eyes onto the felt face. Next, stitch the black eyes onto the white parts. Finally, stitch the nose onto the face.

b. Using 6 strands of black floss, sew a vertical line of backstitches approximately ⅜ inch long under the center of the nose. Then, again using backstitches, embroider a curved mouth at the base of the line you just stitched.

c. Attach the face to the body with blanket stitches worked with 6 strands of brown floss.

step 2. sew the body

a. With **right** sides of the two body pieces facing together and the edges aligned, pin around the edges. Insert the ears at the top of the head as marked on the pattern, being sure to place them *upside down and in between the two body pieces* so that they will flip up when you turn the body **right** side out.

b. Machine stitch around the body with a ¼-inch seam allowance, leaving an opening of 2 to 3 inches at the side of the head to allow for turning the body **right** side out.

c. Before turning the body **right** side out, clip into the seam allowances around the curved seams on the arms, legs, and head, making sure not to clip into the stitching. *(See page 11 for tips on dealing with curves.)*

d. Turn the dog **right** side out, and stuff it with fiberfill. As you stuff it, add some weighted filler to his arms and legs to help define them.

step 3. attach the collar

a. Place the collar around Lucky's neck, and overlap the edges to make sure it fits snugly (the collar's length may vary a bit, depending on how tightly you stuff the dog).

b. Sew a button on one end of the collar, and cut a small slit in the other end for a buttonhole. Then button Lucky's collar.

treeling

DIFFICULTY LEVEL : easy   **FINISHED SIZE** : 8 inches wide by 11 inches high   **SEW** : by machine and hand

Start a softie forest with this turquoise tree, and then design your
own softie animals and flowers to inhabit it. A piece of mirrored
glass would make a perfect lake. Fake spray snow, anyone?

embroidery stitches

backstitch

whipstitch

*Note: When sewing with floss, use
2 strands unless otherwise noted.*

materials

FELT: multicolored scraps for
the leaves; 1 sheet of turquoise
for the treetop; scrap of white for
the eyes; 1 sheet of brown for the
tree trunk

FLOSS: black; pink

THREAD: blue; brown

TOPSTITCHING THREAD: color
that contrasts with leaves

TRIM: 2 black beads for eyes

OTHER: fabric glue

*Note: See page 8 for the list of basic
supplies needed for all projects.*

cut from pattern

FROM FELT
2 turquoise treetops

cut freehand

FROM FELT
19 pointed-oval leaves in various
colors, with a mixture of small
leaves (⅝ by 1 inch) and large
leaves (¾ by 1¾ inches)

2 white eye circles, each ⅞ inch
in diameter

1 brown tree trunk, 4 by
6½ inches (Fold the felt sheet
in half to cut this rectangle, mea-
suring the rectangle with one
end of the pattern positioned
on the fold. Once you sew the
sides of the trunk, the fold will
become the bottom of the trunk.)

continued

sew

*Note: Usually, when sewing by machine, you'll align the pieces and sew them with **right** sides together, and then turn the finished softie **right** side out. But for this project the pieces are aligned with **wrong** sides together, so the ¼-inch seam allowances show on the **right** side and serve as a decorative touch. We don't need to turn the project since it's already **right** side out.*

step 1. attach leaves to the treetop

a. Position the leaves randomly on the treetop, and lightly glue them in place.

b. Using a contrasting color of topstitching thread in your machine, stitch down the center of each leaf to define it. Leave long thread tails at the beginning and end of your stitching, and then pull the tails to the other side of the felt and knot off for a clean finish. Alternatively, you can backstitch by hand, using contrasting topstitching thread down the center of the leaf to get the same effect.

step 2. sew the treetop

a. Place the two halves of the treetop with **wrong** sides together and the edges aligned, and pin together. Machine stitch around the treetop's edges with a ¼-inch seam, leaving a 4-inch opening at the bottom for inserting the trunk.

b. Stuff the treetop three-quarters full with fiberfill.

step 3. put a face on the tree trunk

a. Sew a black bead in the center of each white eye circle.

b. Position the eyes on the trunk, and lightly glue them in place. Then hand sew straight, rather than slanted, whipstitches around each eye with black floss.

c. Create the mouth by hand sewing a few long stitches in pink floss.

step 4. sew the tree trunk

a. Because you cut the trunk on the fold of the fabric, the cut piece, unfolded, will be twice the trunk's length, or 13 inches long. By eliminating a seam on the base of the tree trunk and instead using the fold as the trunk's bottom, the tree will have a smooth, rounded base that does not need to be sewn.

b. To sew the sides of the cut trunk, refold the felt in half at the midpoint, with the short ends aligned and **right** sides together, and machine sew a ¼-inch seam down each side, leaving the top of the trunk open.

c. Turn the trunk **right** side out, and stuff it with fiberfill.

step 5. put it all together

a. Insert the top of the trunk into the opened gap at the bottom of the treetop, and hand stitch the pieces together using a backstitch and thread in the same color you used to sew the treetop. Make the size of your hand stitches as consistent as possible, matching the machine sewn stitches in length. As you stitch, fill in any gaps in the stuffing by adding more.

ARTIST BIO

Lynda Lye

LITTLEODDFOREST
www.forestprints.com

Grew up: Singapore

Creative influences: Lynda grew up doodling and making things with scissors. With a BFA from the School of the Art Institute of Chicago, she dabbles in everything artistic.

Why she makes what she makes: Lynda is inspired by fairy tales and fantasy, and she loves enchanted forests filled with magical animals and scary monsters. She has a special fondness for her treeling design, which she hopes will make the world a friendlier place.

ms. green tea bag

DIFFICULTY LEVEL : moderate   **FINISHED SIZE** : 2½ inches wide by 3 inches high   **SEW** : by machine and hand

Fitted with lots of adorable details, this softie even has its own tea bag label, complete with gray floss "staples." If you like, substitute different color felt to represent other tea blends—black felt for English breakfast tea, gray for Earl Grey, or pale gold for chamomile.

embroidery stitches

backstitch

running stitch

satin stitch

Note: When sewing with floss, use 6 strands unless otherwise noted.

materials

FELT: 1 sheet of moss green for the tea bag face; scrap of pink for the cheeks; 1 sheet of white for the tea bag body and label

FLOSS: black; light pink; green; dark pink; white; gray (see tip on page 42)

THREAD: white; green

TRIM: bead for nose

OTHER: fabric glue

Note: See page 8 for the list of basic supplies needed for all projects.

cut from patterns

FROM FELT

1 white tea bag body

1 green tea bag face

cut freehand

FROM FELT

2 pink cheek circles, each ¾ inch in diameter

2 white tea bag tags, each 1 by 1½ inches

continued

sew

step 1. make the face

a. Embroider the eyes on the green tea bag face, using a backstitch and black floss.

b. Position the cheeks above the fold, and lightly glue them under the eyes.

c. Attach the cheeks to the tea bag face with a running stitch, using light pink floss.

d. Sew on a bead for the nose using green floss.

step 2. make the tea bag tag

a. Embroider the word *tea* in the center of one of the tag pieces, using a backstitch and black floss.

b. On the second tag piece, embroider a heart outline with a backstitch using dark pink floss. Fill in the heart with a satin stitch using green floss.

c. With **right** sides facing, pin the tag pieces together. Make sure that both sides are in the same upright position.

d. Using white thread, machine sew the two tag pieces together, leaving a ⅛-inch seam allowance. Trim any uneven edges.

step 3. assemble the tea bag

a. Lay the white tea-bag body flat, and position the green tea-bag face (with the face showing) on top of the white piece in between the placement lines. This leaves approximately 1¼ inches of white felt at the top and bottom. *Note: The bottom end of the white piece has the extra fold-over edge.*

b. Machine sew near the top and bottom edges of the green piece, attaching it to the white piece underneath.

c. With **right** sides facing, fold the tea bag at the fold line, and machine sew the vertical sides of the tea bag together. Leave the top of the tea bag open for stuffing.

d. Clip the curves, and turn the tea bag **right** side out. Use a crochet hook or another small pointed object to turn out the corners smoothly.

e. Stuff the tea bag with fiberfill.

f. Machine sew the top of the white pieces closed, stitching close to the edge of the front white piece and leaving the tab on the back extending above the stitching line (the tab will be folded over in the next step).

step 4. attach the tag to the tea bag

a. Cut a 12-inch piece of white 6-strand embroidery floss. Thread your embroidery needle, and knot the 6 strands.

b. Insert the needle at the X point on the inside of the flap, shown on the pattern. Sew through the tea bag to the back, and then sew over the top of the tab and through it. This will close the tab. Your stitches will now be on the top of the tap. Repeat, and loop through the top of the stitching (top of the bag), creating a single knot to secure. *Do not cut the remaining floss.*

c. Leaving 6 inches of floss between the bag and the tag, take a couple of ⅛-inch stitches in place through the top of the tag (making sure the word *tea* is right side up), and knot the floss. Then cut the floss to leave a tail of approximately ⅝ inch. Now the tag is attached to your tea bag, just like the real thing.

ARTIST BIO

Heather Pudewa

WREN ELEVEN
www.wreneleven.com

– – – – – – – – – – –

Grew up: In a shack on a coffee plantation in Hawaii and on a ranch in Montana

Creative influences: Fashion design, sewing, and pattern-making classes in college inspired her creativity.

Why she makes what she makes: Heather began to make softies after reading about a plush-toy maker in a magazine. When designing, she tries to capture the unexpected charm in everyday objects. She hit upon the idea of making a tea bag softie while having a cup of tea with a friend.

tramp heart bear

DIFFICULTY LEVEL : moderate   **FINISHED SIZE** : 10¾ inches wide by 16½ inches high   **SEW** : by machine and hand

At first glance, this little guy seems to be just an ordinary bright-colored bear, but look a little closer and you'll see his scars. Cute yet slightly alarming, he gets his edgy, fun look from the contrasting floss that highlights the stitches.

embroidery stitches

running stitch

Note: When sewing with floss, use 6 strands unless otherwise noted.

materials

FELT: 2 sheets of baby blue and 2 sheets of lime green for the body parts; 2 sheets of red for the ears, nose, eyes, heart, and leg decorations

FLOSS: red; light blue

THREAD: red; blue

TRIM: 1 red button for the heart, ⅝ inch in diameter; 1 small red button for the belly button, ½ inch in diameter; 2 blue buttons for eyes, ⅝ inch in diameter

OTHER: pinking shears

Note: See page 8 for the list of basic supplies needed for all projects.

cut from patterns

FROM FELT

2 lime bodies

1 lime small heart, trimmed with pinking shears

1 blue medium heart, trimmed with pinking shears

1 red big heart, trimmed with pinking shears

2 blue heads

2 red inner ears

4 lime outer ears

4 blue legs

4 blue arms

cut freehand

FROM FELT

1 blue belly oval, 4¼ by 5¾ inches

1 red nose oval, 1⅛ by ¾ inches

1 lime muzzle oval, 2⅝ by 1⅞ inches

2 red inner eye ovals, ⅞ by ⅝ inches

2 lime outer eye ovals, 1¼ by 1½ inches

12 red leg stripes, 2⅛ by 1⅛ inches

continued

sew

*Note: With most projects that are machine sewn, the pieces are sewn with **right** sides facing. By contrast, this softie is sewn with **wrong** sides facing, which creates a decorative ¼-inch seam allowance around the edge since the softie is not turned inside out.*

step 1. assemble the front of the body

a. Center the blue belly oval on one of the lime body pieces, and machine sew the two together with red thread, topstitching about ¼ inch from the edge of the blue oval. *(See page 11 for an explanation of topstitching.)*

b. Add a row of embroidered ⅜-inch-tall cross stitches around the belly for a decorative touch, centering the cross stitches over the machine sewn topstitching.

c. Embroider the small lime heart on top of the medium blue heart with a running stitch using red floss.

d. Attach the heart pair sewn in step 1c to the large red heart, using a running stitch and red floss.

e. Embroider the heart set to the belly with a running stitch and light blue floss.

f. Sew the larger red button to the lime heart with blue thread.

g. Using blue thread, sew the smaller red button on the belly for a belly button. Set the front body aside.

step 2. assemble the face

a. Position the red nose on the lime muzzle. Using red thread, machine stitch the two together close to the nose's cut edge.

b. Place the muzzle on the front head piece and machine stitch together with red thread.

c. Position an inner red eye on each lime eye oval, and attach each pair by embroidering a running stitch in blue floss close to the edge of the red oval.

d. Place each eye onto the front head piece and machine stitch around the edge with red thread.

e. Sew the blue buttons in the center of the red ovals for eyes.

f. To make the scar decoration, embroider one long, horizontal straight stitch (about ⅞ inch wide) over the bear's right eye with red floss and 3 perpendicular stitches (⅜ inch or so) on top of the horizontal stitch. Set the face aside.

step 3. assemble the ears

a. Position each red inner ear over a lime ear piece. Using red thread, machine sew each ear pair together close to the red oval's cut edge.

b. Hand embroider a ¾-inch cross stitch on each ear, using blue floss.

c. With **wrong** sides facing, sew the back of each lime ear to the front lime ear with red thread, leaving the bottom edge (where ears will attach to the head) open for stuffing.

d. Stuff each ear with fiberfill and set aside.

step 4. assemble the legs

a. Position and pin 3 red stripes on each of the 4 leg pieces. Be careful to align the red stripes on the front and back of each leg. (See page 9 for a clear picture of the leg stripes.)

b. Machine sew the stripes to each leg piece, stitching close to the cut edge around the perimeter of each stripe.

c. With **wrong** sides facing, match a front and back leg together, aligning the stripes. Pin the aligned leg pieces, and machine sew them together about ¼ inch from the cut edge, leaving an opening at the top of the leg for stuffing.

d. Repeat step 4c to make the second leg.

e. Stuff each leg and set them aside.

step 5. assemble the arms

a. With red floss, embroider the right front arm with two big cross stitches about ¾ inch long.

b. Again using red floss, embroider scar stitches on the left front arm like those you stitched above the bear's right eye in step 2f.

continued

ARTIST BIO

Lisa Martin

www.picturetrail.com/feyprincess

- - - - - - - - - -

Grew up: Texas and Oklahoma

Creative influences: Inspired by artists like Gustav Klimt, Erté, Mark Ryder, and Junko Mizuno, Lisa has an affinity for mixing the cute and the grotesque.

Why she makes what she makes: Lisa began drawing as a small girl and, encouraged by a proud grandfather, progressed to painting, collage, and mixed media. Lisa taught herself to sew and discovered a new outlet for her creativity when she made her first softie as an accessory to go along with a Halloween costume.

c. Machine sew the arm fronts to the arm backs, using red thread and leaving the end that will attach the arms to the body open for stuffing.

d. Stuff the arms and set them aside.

step 6. attach the ears to the head

a. Position the ears between the two head pieces, and pin the ears and head together.

b. Machine sew around the head about ¼ inch from the cut edges using red thread, attaching the ears as you stitch and leaving the neck open for stuffing.

c. Stuff the head and set it aside.

step 7. attach the arms and legs to the body

a. Position and pin the arms and legs in between the front and back body pieces.

b. Machine sew the body front and back together, using red thread and stitching ¼ inch from the cut edges. Make sure the arms and legs are held firmly in place as you stitch around the body, and leave the neck open for stuffing.

c. Stuff the body.

step 8. attach the head and body

a. Insert the head into the body, and attach the two using red floss by hand embroidering them together with straight stitches (½ inch or so).

heartfelt bunny

DIFFICULTY LEVEL : moderate   **FINISHED SIZE** : 1 inch wide (at the bottom) by 3½ inches high   **SEW** : needle felt

This bunny (made with a technique called needle felting) has so much personality that I almost expect her to wink at me. She would be a great gift for Valentine's Day—add a tiny ribbon with a small envelope attached and a secret message inside, and you'll have your true love's heart.

materials

WOOL ROVING: white; pink; green

TRIM: 2 black beads

THREAD: black.

OTHER: foam pad (for working surface, approximately 8 by 10 inches and 3 to 4 inches thick); felting needle

Note: See page 8 for information on wool roving and felting needles and for the list of basic supplies needed for all projects.

continued

needle felt

step 1. make the body

a. Form the body by rolling several strips of white wool into a cylinder approximately 3 inches long.

b. Using the foam pad as a work base, begin felting by gently stabbing the felting needle into the wad of white wool in a random pattern. Stabbing the wool will compress it and make it firmer to the touch.

c. Rotate the wool as you stab to help shape the body. The more you stab it, the closer the fibers become and the more the wool begins to take shape.

d. Layer more strips of wool one at a time to increase the thickness. Keep stabbing and adding wool until you're satisfied with the size, shape, and firmness. At the bottom of the body, fold the loose wool inward, and felt it into the body.

e. Continue stabbing and turning the body to work it until you are satisfied with the shape, which should taper at the neck and widen at the base. Depending on how hard and fast you stab it, it may take you 20 minutes or more to form the body. When finished, set the body aside.

step 2. make the head

a. Form the bunny head by winding strips of white wool into an egg shape.

b. Needle felt the wool until you are satisfied with the shape and it is firm. Set it aside.

step 3. make the nose, ears, tail, and collar, and attach them

a. For the nose, put a small piece of pink wool on the foam pad, and stab it with the needle until it felts. Cut a tiny square out of the felted wool for the bunny's nose.

b. For the first ear, roll a bit of white wool into a rabbit ear shape, and needle felt it, leaving a little bit of loose and unfelted wool at the bottom part of the ear for attaching and blending it into the head. Needle felt a little bit of pink wool onto the center of the ear. Repeat this process to make the second ear.

continued

---

tips

· Needle felting, a very forgiving technique, is akin to working with clay—you're molding and shaping the wool until you're happy with the look.

· The felting needle is extremely sharp, so do be careful. The foam pad is a good work surface and protects your table and the needle, as well as your fingers.

· Sometimes the process of methodically stabbing and stabbing can be soothing— a little bit like yoga for your hands!

ARTIST BIO

Karen Tucker

KRAF-O-LA
www.kraf-o-la.squarespace.com

- - - - - - - - - - - - -

Grew up: The Philippines

Creative influences: Karen was inspired early on by her mother's treasure trove of fabric and beads; by her sister, whose inventive and resourceful nature enables her to make "anything out of anything"; and, eventually, by her classes in fine arts and her career in graphic design.

Why she makes what she makes: Karen started out working with paper and by the age of six had created a line of birthday cards. She lets serendipity play a part in her needle felting, so she is inspired by a bird flying past the window or an elephant dancing on TV.

c. For the bunny's tail, needle felt a small piece of white wool to make a small, round bump.

d. For the collar, needle felt a piece of green wool until you have a strip approximately ¾ inch wide and long enough to fit around the top part of the bunny's body.

e. Attach each piece by needle felting it onto the head or body.

step 4. attach the eyes

a. Sew each bead eye onto the head with black thread.

step 5. make the mouth

a. The mouth is merely an indentation in the bunny's head made by needle felting a tiny area under his nose. The process of stabbing the area compresses the wool even further to make the indentation.

step 6. attach the head to the body

a. Pin the head to the body.

b. Insert the felt needle through the top of the head and deep into the body. Repeat several times.

c. Needle felt around the edges where the head meets the body so that it is firmly attached.

step 7. create the heart

a. Put a small wad of pink wool on the foam pad and poke it several times.

b. Shape the wool into a heart shape by poking around the edges.

c. Attach the heart to the body by stabbing it together.

double scoop

DIFFICULTY LEVEL : challenging   **FINISHED SIZE** : 8½ inches wide by 13 inches high (excluding cherry)   **SEW** : by machine and hand

Big and plushy, this double-scoop mint-chocolate-chip ice cream cone softie makes a really cute pillow. It is one of the more challenging sewing projects but well worth the extra effort.

embroidery stitch

whipstitch

materials

FABRIC: ¼ yard tan plaid cotton for the cone; ¼ yard mint green fleece for the ice cream

FELT: scrap of white for the teeth; scrap of black for the eyes

TRIM: 4 26-mm googly eyes, approximately 1 inch in diameter; 1 red pom-pom, 2 inches in diameter; 29 black pom-poms, ½ inch in diameter

THREAD: matching all-purpose thread for the cone and scoops; light green upholstery thread for the ruffle and all hand sewing

OTHER: hot-glue gun; nylon stocking; weighted filler

Note: See page 8 for the list of basic supplies needed for all projects.

cut from patterns

FROM COTTON

1 plaid cone body

1 plaid cone bottom

1 plaid cone middle

1 plaid cone top

FROM FLEECE

2 mint-green ice cream ruffles

6 mint-green bottom scoops

6 mint-green top scoops

2 white teeth

cut freehand

FROM FELT

4 black eye circles, 1¼ inches in diameter

continued

sew

Note: Use a ⅜-inch seam allowance.

step 1. make the cone

a. With **right** sides facing, align and pin together the two short ends of the cone body. Machine sew a seam along these ends to join them.

b. With **right** sides facing, pin the cone bottom onto the lower (shorter) edge of the cone body, and machine sew the two together.

c. With **right** sides facing, align and pin the smaller-diameter edge of the middle cone circle to the upper edge of the cone body. Machine sew the two edges together.

d. With **right** sides facing, align, pin, and machine sew the short ends of the cone top together.

e. With **right** sides facing, align and pin the upper edge of the cone middle to the lower edge of the cone top. Machine sew the two together.

step 2. make the bottom ruffle

a. With **right** sides facing, sew the short ends of a ruffle together.

b. Fold the loop in half lengthwise, with **wrong** sides facing, the edges aligned, and the raw seam on the inside of the ungathered ruffle.

c. Cut a length of upholstery thread that's a couple inches longer than the loop of the ungathered ruffle, thread your needle, and leave the thread unknotted. Stitching through both aligned edges together, take ¼-inch-long, straight hand stitches close to the raw edges, working around the entire loop, leaving a several-inch-long thread tail at the beginning of your stitching. When you reach the starting point, do not knot the thread, but do leave a long thread tail.

d. Pull the thread tight to gather the loop into a ruffle, adjusting the gathers to evenly space them along the thread and to match the circumference of the top of the ice cream cone body.

e. Tie the thread tails from the beginning and end of your stitches into a knot to secure the adjusted ruffle, and trim the loose ends of the thread.

f. With **right** sides facing and the ruffle positioned to show on the cone's **right** side, pin the ruffle to the top edge of the cone, and machine sew them together fairly close to the edge so that the stitching will not show when you attach the ice cream scoops later. Set the ruffled cone aside.

step 3. make the ice cream scoop

a. With **right** sides facing, align and machine sew the long edges of the first and second sections of the bottom scoop.

b. Continue adding the four remaining sections, sewing each piece in turn, but leave the final section unattached on one edge (you will sew this seam later).

continued

step 4. add facial details on the bottom scoop, and finish the scoop

a. Pick a section to be the scoop's face. Position and machine stitch one set of teeth on this center section, using a zigzag stitch.

b. Position and machine sew one black eye circle on each of the two neighboring sections of the face, using a zigzag stitch.

c. Hot glue a googly eye on each black eye.

d. With **right** sides facing, align and machine sew the last two edges of the scoop to close it, starting from the top edge, sewing down the seam 1½ inches, and stopping. Then take the scoop out from under the needle and reposition it to start sewing the seam from the bottom edge, again sewing 1½ inches toward the center of the seam and stopping. You'll use the 2-inch gap you created in the middle of the seam later for turning the final assembled ice cream cone **right** side out and stuffing it.

step 5. make and attach the second ruffle

a. Repeat steps 2a through 2e to make the second ruffle.

b. With **right** sides facing and the ruffle positioned to show on the scoop's **right** side, pin the ruffle to the top edge of the bottom scoop, and machine sew them together fairly close to the edge so that the stitching will not show when you attach the top scoop later.

step 6. make the top scoop

a. Repeat step 3a to start making the top scoop.

b. Add one more section so that you have three panels of the top scoop sewn together.

c. Sew the other three panels together in the same fashion so that you have two sections. (The reason for making two sections of three panels each rather than joining all six sections at once is that a three-panel section is flatter and much easier to work with when you're sewing on this scoop's facial features.)

d. Center the top scoop's face on one of the top scoop sections. Position and machine stitch one set of teeth on this center section, using a zigzag stitch.

e. Finish adding facial details to the top scoop, following the directions in steps 4b and 4c.

f. With **right** sides facing, align and machine sew the front and back sections of the scoop to close it, starting from the bottom edge and sewing around the top and back down to the bottom on the other side.

step 7. finish assembling the ice cream cone

a. With the top scoop turned **wrong** side out and the bottom scoop turned **right** side out, place the bottom scoop inside the top scoop (the scoops' **right** sides will be facing), and align the seams. Pin the lower edge of the top scoop to the top edge of the bottom scoop, and machine sew the two together.

b. With the double scoop turned **wrong** side out and the cone turned **right** side out, place the cone inside the double scoop (the double scoop and cone will now have **right** sides facing). Then align, pin, and machine sew the bottom edge of the double scoop to the top edge of the cone.

c. Turn the assembled ice cream cone **right** side out through the gap in the final seam on the bottom scoop.

d. Fill the toe of a nylon stocking with enough weighted filler to fill the bottom of the cone, approximately ¾ cup.

e. Tie a knot in the stocking, cut the stocking off above the knot, and insert the filled stocking into the cone bottom through the opening on the bottom scoop.

f. Stuff the rest of the ice cream cone with fiberfill, making sure to stuff it firmly, especially at the bottom, in order to hold the weighted filler in place.

g. Using the green upholstery thread, hand sew the opening in the seam closed with a whipstitch. After tying a knot, sew the ends of the thread into the ice cream, as close to the knot as possible, and out again at least a few inches away from the knot. Pull the thread tight, and cut the trailing end off. This creates a nearly invisible stitch.

h. Hot glue a cherry pom-pom on top.

i. Hot glue the black pom-poms randomly all over the ice cream scoops.

ARTIST BIO

Jenny Harada
www.jennyharada.com

- - - - - - - - - - - -

Grew up: Upstate New York

Creative influences: Jenny's inspirations include Jim Henson's Muppets; Dr. Seuss's book illustrations; Sid and Marty Krofft, producers of children's TV programs in the 1970s; and Tim Burton's films.

Why she makes what she makes: Jenny's designs have a childlike innocence to them. "I never grew out of my toys," she says, "and I often find grown-up stuff boring. Today everything I create is wacky, whimsical, and weird!"

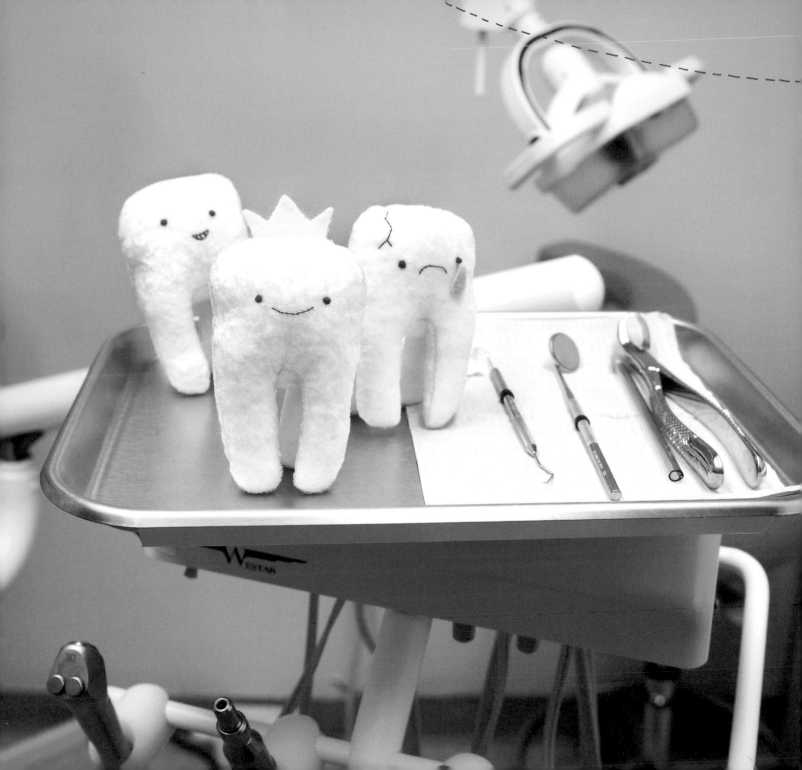

tooth with a crown

DIFFICULTY LEVEL : challenging   **FINISHED SIZE** : 3¼ inches wide by 4½ inches high   **SEW** : by machine and hand

Inspired by a visit to the dentist, this softie reminds us that every-day objects—and even body parts—make great plush toys! Also pictured are Sweet Tooth and Tooth with a Cavity.

embroidery stitches

satin stitch

backstitch

whipstitch

materials

FABRIC: ¼ yard stretchy crushed velvet (or velour) in frosty white

FELT: scrap of yellow for the crown

THREAD: navy for face details; white for the body

Note: See page 8 for the list of basic supplies needed for all projects.

cut from patterns

FROM STRETCHY CRUSHED VELVET OR VELOUR

2 frosty white bodies

2 frosty white inner legs

FROM FELT

1 yellow crown

continued

ARTIST BIO

Teresa Levy

SEWING STARS
www.sewingstars.com

─ ─ ─ ─ ─ ─ ─ ─ ─ ─

Grew up: Southern California

Creative influences: Teresa's crafty mother encouraged her artistic interests, leading her to attend an arts high school and earn a degree in illustration from the Rhode Island School of Design.

Why she makes what she makes: As a child, Teresa made her first softie based on a cartoon character using scraps of fabric left over from her mother's quilting projects. Today she's an illustrator and often uses her artwork as the basis for her softie designs.

sew

step 1. embroider the face

a. Using navy thread, embroider a satin stitch for each eye, and take a few backstitches to make a curved mouth on one of the tooth body pieces.

step 2. make the body

a. With **right** sides facing, machine sew the front and back pieces of the tooth body, starting at one side, sewing about 2¼ inches toward the top of the tooth, and stopping. Take the partially joined pieces out from under the needle, and reposition them to start stitching from the other side of the tooth body. Again, sew about 2¼ inches toward the top of the tooth and stop. You have created an opening at the top, which you'll use later to turn the assembled tooth **right** side out and stuff it.

b. With **right** sides facing, align and machine sew the two inner-leg pieces together at the top.

c. With **right** sides facing, spread open the joined inner-leg piece and align it with the tooth body.

d. Pin **right** sides together, and sew the tooth body down the sides and through the curve of the legs.

e. Notch any excess fabric in the seam allowances around the leg curves. *(See page 11 for tips on dealing with curves.)*

f. Turn the assembled tooth **right** side out through the opening in the top seam, and stuff it firmly with fiberfill.

g. For the Tooth with a Crown, insert the felt crown into the opening on the top seam, and hand sew the opening closed and the crown in place with tiny whipstitches.

h. If the legs seem to splay out a bit, pull up the fabric on the inside base of each leg, and hand sew a dart across the base of each leg. Do this by grabbing a little bit of fabric on one side of the leg with your needle and then a little bit of fabric on the other side, and pulling up the thread to gather up the excess fabric. Work your way across the base of each leg this way to make your tooth tight.

luella bear and her baby bear

DIFFICULTY LEVEL : moderate   **FINISHED SIZE** : **SMALL BEAR** 1½ inches arm to arm by 2¾ inches high   **SEW** : Needle felt and machine
BIG BEAR 2½ inches arm to arm by 4½ inches high   sew the skirt

Tiny needle felted bears are getting to be as popular as their larger teddy bear cousins, and their size makes them small enough to use as a charm for your cell phone or iPod. The instructions for the small bear follow; to make the larger bear, adapt the instructions by adding more wool roving to each piece until they match the measurements for the bigger bear.

embroidery stitch

satin stitch

materials

WOOL ROVING: white

FABRIC: scrap of printed cotton for skirt

FELT: scrap of yellow for suspenders and hair bow

FLOSS: brown for nose, mouth, and paws

THREAD: black cotton thread; upholstery thread (any color)

TRIM: 2 black beads for eyes; 3 small buttons, ¼ inch in diameter

OTHER: wooden skewer; foam pad (for work surface); felting needle; art marker in pink with a blending pen; 24-inch piece 28-gauge wire

Note: See page 8 for information on wool roving and for the list of basic supplies needed for all projects.

cut freehand

FROM FABRIC

1 skirt, 2 by 3⅝ inches

FROM FELT

2 yellow suspenders, ¼ by 2 inches

1 yellow bow (small scrap of ¼-inch-wide felt tied in a small bow)

continued

needle felt

step 1. make the head

a. Start by winding a tuft of wool roving around a wooden skewer and wrapping it tightly into a tapered cylinder. Pull the cylinder off the skewer, keeping it tightly wound.

b. Place the cylinder on a foam pad, and gently poke the wool with the felting needle, making sure to secure the wispy ends and force them inside.

c. Turn as you felt so you get an even shape. The wool will compress and become firmer as you work.

d. Once you have a firm, oval shape, make the head bigger by wrapping more wool around it, and continue to stab.

e. Continue until the head is firm and shaped nicely.

f. To make the pink cheeks, use a permanent colored art marker with a blending pen: apply the color to the cheeks, and immediately apply the colorless blender to soften and diffuse the lines. Set the body aside.

step 2. make and attach the ears

a. Wrap a small piece of white wool into a ball shape, and gently stab until you have a firm ball.

b. Cut the ball in half with fabric scissors. Each half is one ear.

c. Place each ear on the top and slightly to the side of the head.

d. Attach each ear by stabbing it into the head with the felting needle.

e. To form a slight indentation in the center of each ear, just stab a few times in that spot.

step 3. make and attach the muzzle

a. Wrap a small piece of wool into another ball shape. Felt the ball with the felting needle until you have a nicely shaped muzzle.

b. Attach the muzzle to the head by stabbing it on, as you did with the ears.

continued

step 4. add the eyes

a. Thread a sewing needle with a single strand of black thread, knotted at one end. Insert the needle through the bottom of the head, embedding the knot in the head.

b. Bring the needle out at the place where you want the first eye to be, thread a bead onto the needle, and secure the bead tightly, stitching through it a couple of times and then pulling the needle back out through the neck.

c. Repeat steps 3a through 3b to make the second eye.

d. Trim the thread—don't worry if a little shows, you can always use your felting needle to stab it down out of sight.

step 5. embroider a mouth and nose

a. Using brown floss, satin stitch a small nose, and add a pair of diagonal straight stitches leading down from the nose for the mouth.

step 6. make the body

a. Wind a tuft of wool around the wooden skewer, wrapping it tightly into an oval torso shape. Pull the wool cylinder off the skewer, keeping it tightly wound.

b. Place the cylinder on the foam pad, and gently poke the wool with the felting needle, making sure to secure the wispy ends by forcing them inside.

c. Turn the cylinder as you felt to get an even shape.

d. Using the felting needle, stab indentations where the arms and legs will attach to the body so that they will fit together nicely.

step 7. make the arms and legs

a. Set aside an equal amount of wool for each of the two arms and a matching amount of wool for each of the two legs. Wrap each bit of wool around the skewer tightly as before, and then remove it. If you make the two arms one at a time, and then make the two legs one at a time, the resulting arms and legs will probably match better than they would if you made them in random order.

b. Place the wool cylinder on the foam pad, and gently poke it with the felting needle until you have a long tube shape that tapers a bit at the ends.

c. Embroider all four paws with brown floss, making three straight stitches. To do this, use a knotted length of floss, stitch into one paw, and pull the knot inside to bury it before starting your embroidery. When you've finished embroidering, clip the floss, and needle any excess floss into the paw. Then repeat the process on the remaining paws.

step 8. attach the head to the body

a. You'll attach the head with 28-gauge wire to make it secure and able to turn side to side. Thread the wire onto a sewing needle, and tie a knot in one end.

b. Push the needle through the bottom of the torso and up through the head, coming out at the top of the head. Push the needle back down through the torso, and repeat the process a few times until the head is secure.

c. Cut the wire, and bury any excess inside the bear body. Felt, or stab, around the wire, if necessary, to bury it.

d. If there is a small indentation in the top of the bear's head where the wire was "sewn" in and out, cover it up by adding and felting a small tuft of wool.

step 9. attach the arms and legs

a. Thread your sewing needle with a 2-foot-long piece of upholstery thread, but don't knot the ends. Take a stitch into and out of the inside top of one arm, leaving two long equal-length thread tails.

b. Tie both thread tails together tightly in a knot, pulled taut to the arm.

c. Rethread both ends together through the needle's eye, and stitch through the shoulder area of the body, pulling the arm tight to the body and exiting through the other side of the body at the shoulder. (You'll use this single length of thread to attach all four limbs, so there's no need to knot this thread anew at each joint.)

continued

ARTIST BIO

Jenn Docherty

www.jenndocherty.com

- - - - - - - - - -

Grew up: Rural New Jersey

Creative influences: A fascination with miniatures and art history fuels Jenn's creativity, and a felt-making class she took in college set her on the road to learning to make magic out of roving wool.

Why she makes what she makes: Inspired by Japanese craft books and the needle felted bears from the *Anano Café* books (Japanese books featuring adorable needle felted bears), Jenn picked up a needle one day and began jabbing at a piece of roving wool. A tiny bear emerged and she found her craft and her passion.

d. Stitch the thread into and out of the base of the second arm, stitch back into the body, and push the needle down to exit at the opposite hip.

e. Attach the legs as you attached the arms, exiting the needle through the bottom of the body.

f. Tie off the thread, and run the thread tails through the body a few times to securely bury them. Snip off any excess thread, and needle felt any thread tails into the body to bury them.

step 10. make the skirt

a. Fold the cotton fabric in half lengthwise, **right** sides together. Press the fabric if needed.

b. Using a ¼-inch seam allowance, stitch around the three cut sides, leaving a small opening on the last side.

c. Turn the skirt **right** side out through the opening, and edge stitch ⅛ inch from the fold on the last side.

d. Edge stitch the opening closed, and edge stitch around the two remaining sides. Then run a gathering stitch along the top of the skirt. Pull loose thread ends to gather. *(See page 11 for tips on gathering stitches.)*

e. Wrap the skirt around the bear to ensure a good fit. Secure the skirt to the bear with a few small stitches at the top of the skirt.

f. Cut the felt scrap into two suspenders, each about ¼ by 2 inches. Sew a button on one end of each suspender, and then sew the suspenders onto the skirt with the buttons positioned in front. Cross the suspenders in back at the top of the skirt and secure them by sewing on the third button.

step 11. make a bow for the bear

a. Using the small strip of felt left over from the suspenders, make a "bow" by knotting the length once, and sewing it in front of one ear.

party cake

DIFFICULTY LEVEL : easy   **FINISHED SIZE** : 3 inches in diameter by 3½ inches high   **SEW** : by hand

The Mad Hatter would go crazy for this *Alice in Wonderland*–inspired pink cake softie, with its adorable felt dollop of whipped cream on top. If you wish, add beads and sequins or a ribbon around the cake to embellish it further. Because it's made without weighted filler, it's quite light and could be hung as an ornament.

embroidery stitches

whipstitch

French knot

Note: When sewing with floss, use 3 strands unless otherwise noted.

materials

FELT: 1 sheet of pink for frosting; 1 sheet of white for the cake and whipped cream

FLOSS: pink; hot pink; white

TRIM: 1 small, sparkly pom-pom (about the size of a pencil eraser)

Note: See page 8 for the list of basic supplies needed for all projects.

cut from patterns

FROM FELT

1 pink scalloped frosting

5 white triangles for the whipped cream

cut freehand

FROM FELT

1 white cake rectangle, 2 by 10½ inches

2 cake circles (1 pink and 1 white), each 3 inches in diameter

continued

sew

step 1. assemble the side of the cake

a. Pin the scalloped frosting to the white rectangle. Using pink floss, embroider the two together around the scalloped edge with a whipstitch.

b. Add a French knot to the center of each scallop with hot pink floss.

step 2. add the cake top and bottom

a. Pin the side of the cake to the white cake bottom circle, and hand sew together with white floss and a whipstitch.

b. Join the side seams of the cake side together, and whipstitch it closed.

c. Pin and sew the pink cake top on the rest of cake, leaving a 2-inch gap open for stuffing.

step 3. stuff the cake

a. Fill your cake with fiberfill. (No flour, butter, or eggs needed!)

b. Sew the opening closed.

step 4. stabilize the softie

a. Weighted filler is usually added to stabilize a softie. However, this softie designer has a different approach that works well too; Using white floss, sew a loop through the bottom of the cake, up through the top, and back down to the bottom. Pull the stitch tight and knot the ends of the thread together. The resulting dimples on the top (which will be covered by the whipped cream) and underside of the cake help it sit flat.

continued

ARTIST BIO

Aoi Horn

SHINHATSUBAI!
www.shinhatsubai.typepad.com

- - - - - - - - - - - -

Grew up: Okinawa, Japan

Creative influences: Growing up immersed in Japan's "thrifty housewife" and crafting cultures, where the goal was to make cute things that were also functional, gave Aoi plenty of inspiration.

Why she makes what she makes: Aoi (whose poetic name means "blue hollyhock") made this cake softie for a Month of Softies, as part of the *Alice in Wonderland* theme. See page 7 for more information about a Month of Softies.

step 5. make the whipped cream

a. Pin two triangle pieces together.

b. Starting at the top point of the triangle, sew the pair together down one side to the bottom edge.

c. Repeat step 5b, adding the three remaining triangles one at a time, until you've sewn all five pieces.

d. Stuff the whipped cream with fiberfill.

e. Sew the bottom closed.

f. Sew the sparkly pom-pom on top.

g. Sew the whipped cream onto the top of the cake, making sure to stitch under the center of the whipped cream so that your stitches don't show.

portuguese plaid

DIFFICULTY LEVEL : challenging   FINISHED SIZE : 7 inches wide by 6 inches high   SEW : by hand

This plaid pup with "mod" 1960s daisy eyes has a classic look that is reminiscent of Steiff and Dakin stuffed animals from the same period. If you'd like more color, try a brighter plaid in pink and red for a different look.

embroidery stitches

backstitch

whipstitch

blanket stitch

materials

FABRIC: ¼ yard plaid wool for the body; 1 long strip of printed cotton fabric for the collar (about 1¼ by 22 inches)

FELT: 1 sheet of caramel for the underbody, outer eye daisies, and saddle spot; scrap of chocolate brown for top-head gusset; scrap of mustard for neck gusset; scrap of navy for inner eyes; scrap of gray tweed for ears

THREAD: caramel; tan; navy

Note: See page 8 for the list of basic supplies needed for all projects.

cut from patterns

FROM WOOL

2 plaid bodies

FROM FELT

1 brown top-head gusset

1 mustard neck gusset

1 caramel underbody

2 caramel outer-eye daisies

2 gray tweed ears

cut freehand

FROM FELT

1 caramel saddle-spot oval, 1½ by 2⅜ inches

2 navy inner eye circles, ½ inch in diameter

FROM COTTON

1 strip printed cotton collar, 1¼ by 22 inches

continued

sew

step 1. sew the body

a. The body will be sewn together by hand using a backstitch and matching thread. Sew the body pieces in the order given below so that you'll end in the right place with the right edges and points together. Match up fabric points with the letters as shown on the pattern. To begin, with **right** sides facing, pin together and sew one of the body pieces to the top-head gusset—from point A to point B1.

b. With **right** sides facing, pin the second body piece to the other side of the gusset you've just attached, and sew the two sides together from point A to point B1.

c. Sew the neck gusset to the body, from A to B2.

d. Repeat and sew the neck gusset to the other side of the body, again from A to B2.

e. Sew the underbody of the dog to the body, from points C to D on the pattern.

f. Repeat with the second side of the body.

g. Finish sewing the main body pieces together from B1 to D, leaving a 2-inch opening along the top of the back for turning **right** side out and stuffing.

h. Clip the curves, and turn **right** side out. *(See page 11 for tips on dealing with curves.)*

step 2. stuff the softie

a. Stuff, beginning with the head. This softie looks best if it's tightly stuffed, so do your best to get the stuffing into all the small places, paying particular attention to the legs and tail so that he'll be able to stand.

b. Sew the opening closed with a whipstitch.

continued

step 3. add the eyes and saddle spot

a. With a blanket stitch in matching color floss, position the saddle spot on the pup's back, and embroider it on.

b. Embroider the daisy-shaped outer eyes onto face, one on each side of the head.

c. Add the navy eye circles onto the center of each daisy.

step 4. add the ears

a. Position each ear, and whipstitch along the top edge only, leaving the rest of the ear hanging free.

step 5. add the collar

a. Tie a length of printed cotton fabric (or ribbon) around the pup's neck for a collar.

amigurumi pink bunny

DIFFICULTY LEVEL : moderate   **FINISHED SIZE** : **BODY** 1½ inches wide by 3 inches long   **SEW** : crochet and by machine and hand

EARS 1 inch long

ARMS AND LEGS ½ inch long

This sweet bunny is an *amigurumi*—a Japanese word loosely meaning "crocheted toy." Crafting amigurumi is very popular in Japan and is gaining fans in the United States. For a link to an online tutorial, see "Resources" (page 118).

embroidery stitch

French knot

gauge

8 stitches per inch

abbreviations

sc = single crochet

inc = increase

dec = decrease

materials

YARN: pink fingering or baby yarn

FABRIC: scrap of printed cotton (about 1 by 3½ inches)

FLOSS: black for eyes; dark pink for nose

THREAD: to match cloth for skirt

OTHER: size B crochet hook

Note: See page 8 for the list of basic supplies needed for all projects.

cut freehand

FROM PRINTED COTTON
1 skirt, 1 by 3½ inches

continued

crochet

step 1. make the head

Chain 2, 6 sc in 2nd chain from hook.

Round 1: Inc in every sc (12 sc). Mark end of 1st round.

Round 2: Inc in every 2nd sc (18 sc).

Round 3: Inc in every 3rd sc (24sc).

Round 4: Sc in every sc.

Round 5: Inc by 1 sc in 12th and 24th sc (26 sc).

Rounds 6-7: Sc in every sc.

Round 8: Dec in 13th and 26th sc (24 sc).

Round 9: Sc in every sc.

Round 10: Dec in every 4th sc (18 sc).

Round 11: Dec in every 3rd sc (12 sc).

Stuff the head tightly with fiberfill. Embroider each eye with a French knot using 6 strands of black floss. Add a few straight stitches for the bunny's nose and mouth with the pink floss.

step 2. make the body

Continue with crochet.

Round 12: Inc in every 2nd sc (18 sc).

Round 13: Inc in every 6th sc (21 sc).

Rounds 14-16: Sc in every sc.

Round 17: Dec in every 3rd sc (14 sc).

Rounds 18-19: Sc in every sc.

Stuff the body tightly with fiberfill. Draw up the bottom of the body, and secure it tightly.

continued

---

tips

- Make sure your bunny is tightly crocheted so that the stuffing will not show through. If you are a loose crocheter, you may need to use a hook that is one size smaller than the one called for in the project instructions.

- The arms, legs, and ears are not stuffed—they are small enough to stand up nicely on their own.

step 3. make the ears

Chain 2, 6 sc in 2nd chain from hook (6 sc).

Work 6 rounds sc in every sc.

Repeat and make the second ear.

Finish off, leaving a long tail.

Position the ears on the head and sew them in place, using the tail end of the yarn.

step 4. make the arms and legs

Chain 2, 6 sc in 2nd chain from hook (6 sc).

Work 4 rounds sc in every sc.

Repeat, making the second arm and two legs.

Position the arms and legs on the body, and sew them into place.

step 5. make the skirt

a. Fold the fabric in half with **right** sides facing, and align the short raw edges.

b. Machine stitch a seam along the matched raw edges, turn the skirt **right** side out, and fold over a very small hem on the top raw edge for a waistband.

c. Place the skirt on the bunny, positioning the seam at center back. Using a double thread, hand sew the skirt to the bunny.

paper doll dress

This vintage-inspired felt dress softie would make a great party favor for a little girl's birthday celebration. Or omit the stuffing, embroider names onto each dress, and use them as place cards at your next tea party. The materials and instructions below are for the lavender dress with pink rickrack trim.

embroidery stitch

blanket stitch

Note: When embroidering with floss, use 2 strands unless otherwise noted.

materials

FELT: 1 sheet of pale lavender for dress; scrap of mustard yellow for collar

FABRIC: scrap of printed cotton for petticoat and pocket

FLOSS: yellow; lavender

TRIM: 4 inches pink rickrack; 1 pink paper flower; 1 small yellow seed bead; 6 inches pink ribbon, ¼ inch wide

OTHER: fabric glue; pinking shears; wire trimmers or jewelry pliers (optional); 8-inch piece 20-gauge wire, for making hanger (optional)

Note: See page 8 for the list of basic supplies needed for all projects.

cut from patterns

FROM FELT
2 lavender dresses

1 yellow collar

FROM PRINTED FABRIC
1 petticoat

1 pocket

continued

tip

• Substitute a button or large bead for the pink paper flower if you wish.

sew

step 1. decorate the dress front

a. Choose one of the cut felt dress pieces to be the front.

b. Cut out the inverted V as shown on the pattern.

c. Glue the **right** side of the petticoat to the **wrong** side of the dress front, centering the petticoat in the opening. The **right** side of the printed fabric is intended to show through the V.

d. Trim the top of the pocket with pinking shears, and pin the pocket in place on the dress front.

e. Embroider the pocket to the dress using a blanket stitch and the yellow floss. Leave the top of the pocket unsewn—the pinked top edge will keep the fabric from unraveling.

step 2. add rickrack to the dress back

a. Make sure the rickrack length matches the width of the dress hem. Trim it if necessary.

b. Place the dress back on a flat surface, and dab dots of fabric glue along the hem.

c. Glue the rickrack onto the dress back, making sure that half of the scalloped edge shows below the hem.

step 3. assemble the dress

a. Place the dress front and back with **wrong** sides together, and glue the pair together *at the hem only*.

b. Sew the dress pieces together, starting at the hem and up to each armhole, using a blanket stitch and the lavender floss.

c. Leave the top of the dress open for stuffing.

continued

ARTIST BIO

Alicia Paulson

POSIE GETS COZY
www.rosylittlethings.typepad.com

- - - - - - - - - -

Grew up: Chicago

Creative influences: Alicia grew up in an entrepreneurial and artistic family, and she later took a pattern making class in college, which equipped her to follow her inspirations, including English country design, vintage children's toys, and Dover clip-art books.

Why she makes what she makes: Alicia first started a silk ribbon embroidery business filling custom orders for fashion designers, which led to her current design work making one-of-a-kind handbags, vintage-inspired crochet wear, and handmade gifts.

step 4. stuff the dress

a. Stuff the dress lightly up to the waist, just enough to puff out the skirt. Leave the dress unstuffed from the waist up.

step 5. finish the embellishment

a. Attach the paper flower to the collar by sewing a seed bead though its center.

b. Lightly glue the collar around the front neckline.

c. Blanket stitch the collar at the shoulder seams with yellow floss, sewing through all three layers of felt. Do not sew the armholes closed.

step 6. make the hanger (optional)

a. Using a wire trimmer or jewelry pliers, curl the wire into a hanger form, starting at the top hook.

b. The bottom of the hanger should be approximately 2 inches wide—just wide enough to extend a bit past the dress armholes (just like a real hanger).

ice cream sandwich

DIFFICULTY LEVEL : moderate **FINISHED SIZE :** 3½ inches wide by 5¾ inches long by 1¾ inches deep **SEW :** by machine and hand

Too cute to eat, this ice cream sandwich could be part of a picnic gift basket filled with other felt food. Or you could add weighted filler, and it becomes a delicious-looking paperweight for your desk.

embroidery stitches

backstitch

whipstitch

Note: Use 3 strands of floss for mouth.

materials

FELT: 1 sheet of brown for sandwich top and bottom; scrap of black and a scrap of white for eyes

FLEECE: scrap of creamy white for ice cream

FLOSS: red

THREAD: white

OTHER: fabric glue

Note: See page 8 for the list of basic supplies needed for all projects.

cut from pattern

FROM FELT
2 brown sandwich crusts

cut freehand

FROM FLEECE
2 long creamy white ice cream rectangles, 2 by 4¾ inches

2 short creamy white ice cream rectangles, 2 by 2¾ inches

FROM FELT
2 black eye circles, ½ inch in diameter

2 white eye circles, ¾ inch in diameter

continued

sew

step 1. embroider the mouth

a. Using a backstitch and red floss, embroider the mouth on the top crust, positioning it slightly below the center of the crust. Set aside.

step 2. sew the ice cream fleece

a. With **right** sides facing, machine sew the two long and two short pieces of ice cream fleece together to form an open rectangle.

b. Leave the fourth side open for stuffing later.

step 3. put the sandwich together

a. Position the top crust facedown on your work surface, and center the ice cream rectangle on the crust's **wrong** side, with the **right** side of the ice cream fleece facing out. Turn under the raw edges of the ice cream rectangle toward the center of the crust rectangle, and pin through the raw edges to attach the ice cream to the crust.

b. Using white thread, machine sew the raw edges of the ice cream rectangle to the top crust from the *inside,* making sure that the crust's scalloped edges remain unsewn.

c. Turn the ice cream sandwich inside out. The scalloped edges should now be in the middle

d. The next step is to attach the bottom crust. This can be a bit difficult to machine sew, so hand sewing directions as well as those for machine sewing are provided below.

To machine sew: Pin the bottom crust to the cream fleece, carefully tucking the scallops of the bottom crust into the middle so you don't accidentally sew over them. Make sure the corners of the top and bottom crusts line up—this will give your sandwich a clean, rectangular shape.

continued

ARTIST BIO

Heidi Kenney

MY PAPER CRANE
www.mypapercrane.com

- - - - - - - - - - -

Grew up: Germany, Texas, and New England

Creative influences: Heidi's mother made small dolls and quilts, and her father was a painter-sculptor.

Why she makes what she makes: Purses were among Heidi's first fabric creations. One day, while making a handbag, she decided to turn it into a hedgehog with handles, sparking an interest in making nonfunctional plush art. One of Heidi's first softies was a piece of toast.

Sew the crust to the fleece ice cream. As you sew each side, stop for a moment to straighten the softie. You may want to backstitch a bit so the threads don't unravel. Leave the last side open for stuffing.

To hand sew: Turn the ice cream sandwich **right** side out. Position the bottom crust onto the ice cream sandwich, and hand sew the parts together, using a backstitch. Leave the last side open for stuffing.

step 4. stuff the sandwich

a. Turn the sandwich **right** side out (if you've sewn it on a machine). All scallops should be free and not sewn into any seam.

b. Stuff the ice cream with fiberfill through the opening in the fleece ice cream.

step 5. finish

a. Hand sew the last side of the ice cream fleece closed with a whipstitch.

b. Glue the smaller black eye circles onto the larger white eye circles, and then glue the eye sets to the top crust, approximately ¾ inch above the mouth.

brock the builder

DIFFICULTY LEVEL : easy   **FINISHED SIZE** : 7¼ inches wide by 10¼ inches high   **SEW** : by machine and hand

Brock was inspired by a friend of the artist who loves using power tools and watching *Laverne & Shirley*. Brock is asymmetrical—one foot is bigger than the other—which only adds to his unique charm.

embroidery stitch

running stitch

materials

FELT: 2 sheets of orange for body and inner loops of the letter *B*; scrap of black for eyes and letter *B*; scrap of gray for tools; scraps of brown and beige for tool belt

THREAD: orange

OTHER: weighted filler; fabric glue

Note: See page 8 for the list of basic supplies needed for all projects.

cut from patterns

FROM FELT

2 orange bodies

1 brown tool belt

1 gray set of tools

1 black letter *B*

orange inner loops of letter *B*

cut freehand

FROM FELT

2 black eye circles, ⅜ inch in diameter

1 beige buckle, ½ by 1 inch

continued

sew

Note: Use machine thread for all hand sewing.

step 1. make the body

a. With **right** sides facing, place the body pieces together and sew the body, leaving 3 inches open at the top of head for turning and stuffing. Clip the seam allowance around all the curves. *(See page 11 for tips on dealing with curves.)*

b. Turn the body **right** side out, and stuff the arms and legs with weighted filler to add definition to those areas. *(See page 9 for information on working with filler.)*

c. Continue stuffing the body with fiberfill.

d. Hand sew the opening closed, pinching together the two folded edges and using tiny running stitches close to the edge.

step 2. add features

a. Position the eyes, tools, and belt parts on body, and glue them in place.

b. Glue the black *B* to the body, and glue the orange inner loop pieces on top.

lonely dollop

The Lonely Dollop is a blob of poo, and he has a lonely look, says his creator, because he's stinky and therefore has no friends. This softie is fast and simple to sew, and you'll have so much fun making it that you won't think about the smell!

embroidery stitch

whipstitch

materials

FELT: brown for the body; ruby red and white for the eyes; black for the mouth

FLOSS: black

OTHER: fabric glue

Note: See page 8 for the list of basic tools needed for all patterns.

cut from pattern

FROM FELT
2 brown bodies

cut freehand

FROM FELT
2 red inner eye circles, ⅝ inch in diameter

2 white outer eye ovals, ⅞ by 1½ inches

1 black rounded-edge rectangle mouth, ¼ by 4½ inches

continued

tip

* If you prefer to stitch the eyes on, use a blanket stitch, but do this first before sewing the body pieces together.

ARTIST BIO

Shawn Smith

SHAWNIMALS
www.shawnimals.com

- - - - - - - - - - - - -

Grew up: Small town near Chicago

Creative influences: Video games, comic books, and the *Star Wars* films provide Shawn with his creative inspiration.

Why he makes what he makes: Shawn was one of the first art plush-toy design-ers, having started his business in 2001. When developing a new design, he tries to approach a common object with wit and originality. The results are often irreverent and always amusing.

sew

step 1. make the dollop

a. With **right** sides facing, align the edges of the two body pieces and machine sew around the edges, leaving a 3-inch opening at the bottom for turning the dollop **right** side out and stuffing it.

b. Clip the curves, and turn the dollop **right** side out. *(See page 11 for tips on dealing with curves.)*

c. Glue the red inner eye to the white outer eye, and then glue the set to the dollop. Repeat for the second eye.

d. Glue the mouth under the eyes.

e. Stuff the dollop with fiberfill.

f. Hand sew the opening closed with a whipstitch, using black floss.

george the elephant king

DIFFICULTY LEVEL : moderate   **FINISHED SIZE** : 10 ½ inches wide by 19 ½ inches high (ear to ear)   **SEW** : by machine and hand

The first plush toy ever made was an elephant-shaped pincushion sewn by Margarete Steiff in Germany in 1880. Steiff subsequently founded the eponymous company famous for its teddy bears. The style of this elephant is quite different, but it's definitely a descendant of the original softie.

embroidery stitches

backstitch

whipstitch

materials

FABRIC: ¼ yard printed cotton fabric for body

FELT: 4 sheets of gray for head, ears, trunk, arms, and legs; scrap of green for hat; 1 sheet of black for collar (optional)

FLOSS: tan; gold

THREAD: white; gray; black

TRIM: 2 small pearl beads for eyes; 1 small pom-pom for hat; 13 inches narrow ribbon (optional)

OTHER: scalloped-edge scissors (preferably with a small scallop)

Note: See page 8 for the list of basic tools needed for all patterns.

cut from patterns

FROM FELT

2 gray heads

2 gray ears (outer edge trimmed with scalloped-edge scissors)

2 gray arms

1 gray trunk (cut on fold)

2 gray legs (cut on fold)

1 green hat (cut on fold)

FROM PRINTED COTTON

2 bodies

cut freehand

FROM FELT

1 black collar, 2 by 10 inches, with both long edges trimmed with scalloped-edge scissors (optional)

continued

sew

step 1. make the head

a. Using fabric chalk, mark the head darts as shown on the pattern, and machine stitch a dart approximately 2 inches long down the middle of each head piece. (Felt does not have a **right** or **wrong** side, but once you've stitched the dart, the side of the felt with the excess created by the dart becomes the **wrong** side.) Clip the curve along the dart on the **wrong** side, being careful not to cut into the seam. (See page 11 for tips on dealing with curves.)

b. Using white thread, sew the small pearl-bead eyes onto the **right** side of the elephant's face. For the eyebrows, add a few backstitches angled over the eyes using 6 strands of the tan floss. Also embroider a small, curved mouth with a few backstitches in tan floss.

c. With **right** sides facing, place the head pieces together, matching up the darts. Insert the ears inside and in between the head pieces, and pin it all together, referring to the pattern for placement. Machine stitch around the head, leaving the bottom neck edge open.

d. Clip the curved seams, and turn the head **right** side out.

e. Stuff the head firmly with fiberfill, and set it aside.

step 2. make the body

a. Place and pin the arms on the **right** side of the body fabric front, positioning them on a diagonal starting approximately 2½ inches down from the neck. Refer to the pattern for placement lines.

b. Machine sew the arms to the body front with a blanket or zigzag stitch.

c. With **right** sides facing, pin the body front to the body back, and machine stitch them together, leaving the neck edge open.

d. Turn the body **right** side out and stuff it, leaving a ½-inch space at the neck unstuffed.

continued

step 3. attach the head to the body

a. Place the head into the body, and gently work it down into the body cavity about ¾ inch until the widths of the two openings match.

b. Turn under the raw neck edge. Pin and hand sew the head to the body with a whipstitch, using gray thread.

step 4. embellish the trunk with nostrils

a. Lay the trunk piece flat, and determine the midpoint, where it will be folded across its width. Embroider 2 stitches, each ¼ inch long, with gold floss across this center point to create the nostrils, which will show on the front and back of the trunk when it's folded.

step 5. add the trunk

a. Fold the trunk piece at the midpoint with **right** sides facing, and machine stitch the long sides together, leaving the wider top edge open.

b. Turn the trunk **right** side out. *Do not fill it with fiberfill—it is meant to be unstuffed.*

c. Hand sew the top seam closed with a whipstitch, and then hand sew the finished trunk onto the head at a slight angle.

step 6. add the legs

a. With **right** sides facing, machine sew the folded leg sides together, leaving the wider top edge open.

b. Turn each leg **right** side out, and stuff both with fiberfill.

c. Using a whipstitch and gray thread, hand sew the legs closed and onto the body.

step 7. make the party hat

a. Fold and pin the hat in half, with **right** sides facing and the edges matching.

b. Machine sew along the straight edge, leaving the bottom curve open. Sew as close to the edge as possible (with less than a ¼-inch seam allowance). Trim the hat's bottom edge with the scalloped-edge scissors.

c. Turn the hat **right** side out, and sew the small pom-pom on top.

d. Place the hat on George's head, and if you wish, add a few stitches to secure it or use a decorative straight pin to keep it in place.

step 8. make the collar (optional)

a. Fold the black felt collar in half lengthwise, and wrap it around the neck, overlapping it slightly in the back. Trim the excess collar fabric as needed, and hand sew the collar closed.

b. Whipstitch the collar to the neck using black thread.

c. Wrap a narrow ribbon around the collar, and tie it in front.

ARTIST BIO

Trish Millener

SWEETNELLIE
www.sweetnellie.net

- - - - - - - -

Grew up: Wisconsin

Creative influences: Her grandmother and an aunt taught Trish needlework skills. That, combined with her background in photojournalism, lends a strong visual orientation to her softie design work.

Why she makes what she makes: Trish started her crafting business in the fourth grade, making potholders and selling them door to door. Today she gets a kick out of dressing up her pets, she says, "but there's a limit to how far you can go with that. Softies don't complain and they don't bite." Her inspiration? "The simple, clean design of anything . . . and, of course, animals in clothing."

the debutante

DIFFICULTY LEVEL : easy   FINISHED SIZE : 7 inches wide by 10 inches high   SEW : by machine and hand

The single large eye and luxurious fake fur of this softie make it stand out in a crowd. Fur tends to shed a bit as you're working with it, but a little Static Guard will help to keep it from getting in your way.

embroidery stitch

whipstitch

materials

FABRIC: ¼ yard black-and-white-tipped green fake fur; ⅛ yard turquoise fake fur; strip of purple tulle, 4 inches by 1½ yards

THREAD: green; purple

EYE: plastic eye with washer, 28 mm, or approximately 1¼ inches in diameter

OTHER: hair comb; Static Guard (optional)

Note: See page 8 for the list of basic supplies needed for all projects.

cut from patterns

FROM FUR

1 green top front piece

1 turquoise bottom front piece

1 green back piece

continued

ARTIST BIO

Krissy Harris

BIGGER KRISSY
www.biggerkrissy.com

- - - - - - - - - -

Grew up: Los Angeles, California

Creative influences: Krissy is inspired by a wide range of crafting interests, including knitting, crocheting, and making dioramas and collages.

Why she makes what she makes: Krissy's "biggerCritters" are for people who want toys with that extra pop of personality. Krissy's on a mission—she calls her critters "a renegade crew of motley creatures determined to overthrow the long-standing reign of generic, insufferably cute stuffed toys."

sew

step 1. sew the front pieces and attach the front to the back

a. With the **right** sides of the top and bottom front pieces facing and the edges aligned, pin and machine sew the edges together using green thread to create the front's horizontal seam.

b. Placing the **right** sides of the fur together, pin the front and back pieces, and machine sew around the entire softie, leaving a 3-inch opening at the bottom for turning **right** side out and stuffing.

step 2. attach the eye

a. While the body is still inside out, determine the placement of the eye and cut a tiny hole just big enough to secure the eye and washer parts.

b. Attach the washer and eye (the washer will be on the inside and the eye will be on the outside when fabric is turned). Keep the eye 1 inch from the fabric seam, in order to allow the maximum amount of fur to be combed out over the eye.

step 3. stuff and close the softie

a. Turn the softie **right** side out, and stuff it with fiberfill. Err on the side of understuffing this softie. Fold the open edges under a bit, and whipstitch the opening closed.

step 4. add a tulle skirt

a. The tulle is hand sewn to the outside of the softie at the seam line where the green and turquoise fur meet. Begin by pinching a little of the tulle together along the center of the strip and sewing it to the fur body, starting at the left seam.

b. Move across the front, pinching and sewing until you reach the other side seam. Pinch a little or a lot of the tulle to get the look you like.

step 5. comb the fur

a. Gently comb and pull little bits of fur out from the seams around the body. Combing camouflages the seams and gives the softie a nice, fluffy look.

patricia

DIFFICULTY LEVEL : moderate   **FINISHED SIZE** : 17 ¾ inches wide by 22 inches high   **SEW** : by machine and hand

Despite its three separate, alien-like eyes, this softie has a friendly appearance. The different textures of the corduroy, felt, cotton, and lace are fun to work with and easy to sew with your machine. If you plan to hand sew, consider using a combination of felt and fleece in unusual colors.

materials

FABRIC: ¼ yard teal corduroy for head, eyes, and arms; piece of printed cotton for the body, approximately 17 by 15 inches; scrap of green striped cotton for the legs, 6 by 13 inches

FELT: scrap of red for the lips; scrap of yellow for dress placket; scrap of black felt for hands and feet (optional)

THREAD: tan; teal

TRIM: 4 plastic koala bear paws for hands and feet; 3 plastic eyes with washers, 12 mm, or approximately ½ inch in diameter; 13 inches purple lace, 1 inch wide; 2 green square buttons, ¾ inch in diameter; 1 gold plastic star, ⅞ inch in diameter

Note: See page 8 for the list of basic supplies needed for all projects.

cut from patterns

FROM FELT
1 red mouth

FROM CORDUROY
2 heads

4 arms

6 eye ovals

FROM COTTON
2 printed-cotton bodies

4 green-striped legs

cut freehand

FROM FELT
1 yellow dress placket, 1⅝ by 3¼ inches

continued

---

tips

- Patricia's hands and feet are made from plastic koala bear claws purchased at a store in Australia (where the designer lives). You can purchase them online (see "Resources," page 118), but they're not readily available in the United States. You may want to experiment with other materials: cut freehand double or triple layers of felt and then glue or embroider them together, or try small hair combs or hardware store items to give the doll an edgy look.

- Possible substitutions for the plastic star include a child's sheriff's badge or a button.

sew

step 1. sew the felt details onto the face and body

a. Position the red mouth approximately ¾ inch from the bottom edge of one of the heads, and using tan thread, attach it by machine with a narrow zigzag stitch. Sew entirely around the mouth's outside edge and then horizontally across its center.

b. Center the dress placket ½ inch down from the top raw edge of the **right** side of one of the body pieces. Using tan thread, machine sew the placket in place using a decorative or zigzag stitch.

step 2. sew the arms and legs

a. With the **right** sides of two arm pieces facing and the edges aligned, stitch the arm together along its long sides with teal thread, leaving both short ends unsewn.

b. With the arm still turned **wrong** side out, insert one plastic claw between the arm's lower curved fabric edges, aligning the claw's wrist with the arm's fabric edges and with the fingers inside the arm. Machine stitch the claw in place, sewing entirely across the arm's curved lower edge. (A regular needle will sew through these claws. See "Tips" for alternative claw materials.)

c. Turn the arm **right** side out, and stuff it with fiberfill.

d. Repeat steps 3a through 3c for the second arm.

e. Repeat steps 3a through 3c to make the legs, using tan thread instead of teal. Set the arms and legs aside.

step 3. sew the eye ovals

a. With **right** sides facing and the edges aligned, machine sew each pair of eye ovals together with teal thread, leaving open the straight edge where the eye oval will attach to the head.

b. While the eye ovals are still turned **wrong** side out, center and attach a plastic eye and washer to each one—the washer should be on the **wrong** side of the fabric and the plastic eye on the **right** side, so the eye will show when the fabric is turned **right** side out.

c. Turn the eye ovals **right** side out, stuff them lightly, and set aside.

continued

step 4. attach the head to the body

a. On each fabric body piece, turn under to the **wrong** side ½ inch of the top raw edge, and iron the folded edge flat. (The yellow placket will now be at the top edge of the body).

b. With **right** sides facing, place the body front on top of the head front, so that there is a small overlap, and machine stitch the body to the head with tan thread using a decorative or a zigzag stitch.

c. Repeat steps 4a and 4b to attach the back of the head to the back of the body.

d. Attach the purple lace to the bottom edge of the **right** side of the two body pieces with a machine zigzag stitch using tan thread.

step 5. sew the sides of the body

a. With **right** sides of the front and back body facing and the edges aligned, place and pin the arms and eye ovals in position (the arms and eye ovals should extend inside the body cavity at this point). Be sure to position the arms so the front of each hand will face forward once the body is turned **right** side out.

b. Pin the front and back body pieces together with the arms and eyes in position.

c. Starting at the bottom of the body and sewing up the sides, machine stitch with tan thread the sides of the body, catching in the arms and eyes as you sew.

d. Turn the body **right** side out.

step 6. stuff the body, add the legs, and close patricia

a. Stuff the head and body firmly.

b. Insert the legs into the lower edge of the body, making sure that each foot faces forward, and machine sew the bottom closed, using a decorative or a zigzag stitch.

step 7. embellish the dress placket

a. Hand sew the 2 buttons onto the yellow dress placket.

b. Sew the plastic star to one side of the dress placket.

pig/wolf

DIFFICULTY LEVEL : challenging   **FINISHED SIZE** : 15 inches wide by 16½ inches long   **SEW** : by machine and hand

Based on a drawing by one of the artist's children, Pig/Wolf is a fun project to make since each arm, hand, and face is completely different. This softie is a bit challenging to sew since there are more than twenty different pieces, but it's almost like getting two softies in one!

embroidery stitches

whipstitch

backstitch

blanket stitch

French knot

materials

FABRIC: ¼ yard brown velour for wolf head, snout, ears, and arms; ¼ yard pink velour for pig head, snout, ears, and hands and wolf mouth; ¼ yard green-striped jersey for body and wolf and pig sleeves; scrap of pink satin for pig's inner ears; scrap of navy velour for wolf nose

FELT: 1 sheet of white for pig and wolf eyes and wolf teeth

THREAD: Brown, tan, pink, white, black, and green

Note: See page 8 for the list of basic supplies needed for all projects.

cut from patterns

For parts calling for two pieces to be cut, cut one in reverse.

FROM VELOUR

2 brown right ears for wolf

2 brown left ears for wolf

2 pink gums for wolf

2 brown snouts for wolf

1 brown underchin for wolf

2 brown right paws for wolf

2 brown left paws for wolf

2 pink left paws for pig

2 pink right paws for pig

2 brown heads for wolf

2 pink left ears for pig

2 pink right ears for pig

1 pink front snout for pig

1 pink top snout for pig

1 pink bottom snout for pig

2 pink heads for pig

FROM FELT

2 white teeth for wolf

FROM JERSEY

2 green-striped bodies

2 green-striped right wolf sleeves

2 green-striped left wolf sleeves

4 green-striped pig sleeves

FROM SATIN

1 pink left inner ear piece for pig

1 pink right inner ear piece for pig

continued

cut freehand

FROM VELOUR
1 navy nose circle for wolf,
1½ inches in diameter

FROM FELT
1 white left eye oval for wolf,
1½ by 1¼ inches

1 white right eye oval for wolf,
1¼ by ¾ inch

1 white left eye circle for pig,
⅝ inch in diameter

1 white right eye oval for pig,
¾ inch in diameter

sew

step 1. sew the wolf ears

a. With **right** sides facing and the edges aligned, machine sew with brown thread the two pieces of each wolf ear together, leaving the seam open at the base of the ear where it will attach to the head.

b. Turn each ear **right** side out, and machine sew a decorative line about 1 inch long down its vertical center using tan thread. On the larger ear, slightly curve the line of this "inner ear" decoration.

c. Set the ears aside. *Do not stuff the ears.*

step 2. make the wolf snout

a. Pin one of the pink gum pieces onto one of the snout pieces, positioning the gum as marked on the pattern. Using pink thread, machine stitch the pair together, stitching around the gum's outer edge and folding under a very small seam allowance on the gum as you stitch.

b. Repeat step 2a to attach the second gum onto the second snout.

c. Pin one set of teeth on top of the gum on the first snout, aligning the bottom of the teeth with the bottom of the gum. Using white thread, edge stitch the teeth in place. *(See page 11 for an explanation of edge stitching.)* Repeat this step to attach the gum and teeth to the second snout.

continued

d. With **right** sides facing and the edges aligned, sew both snout pieces together at the top seam, and continue stitching down the front of the nose, leaving a small ½-inch opening in the front of the nose between the front teeth.

e. Keeping the snout positioned with **right** sides facing, pin the underchin piece to the snout, aligning the raw edges, again with **right** sides facing, and machine stitch the two parts together.

f. Turn the snout **right** side out, and using a whipstitch and black thread, hand sew the navy nose piece onto the snout. Turn the nose's fabric edges under as you sew, and leave a small opening for stuffing the nose.

g. Stuff the nose, and finish sewing it to the snout.

h. Stuff the snout, and set it aside.

step 3. make the body

a. With **right** sides facing and the edges aligned, machine stitch the striped jersey body pieces together with green thread, leaving all four armholes on these seams open. To leave the armholes open when sewing each seam, you'll need to stitch up to and stop at the top mark for the armhole that you transferred from the pattern. *(See page 10 for information on transferring pattern marks.)* Then lift up the needle and presser foot, and move the fabric to the bottom mark for this armhole, pulling out a little extra thread for a longer thread tail as you move the fabric (the longer thread tails will keep the stitching at each end of the opening from pulling out easily). With the fabric repositioned, lower the needle and presser foot, and continue sewing the seam until you reach the top mark for the second arm. Again lift the presser foot and needle, move the fabric to the second mark for the arm, lower the presser foot and needle, and finish sewing the seam.

b. Repeat for the other side of the body, and set it aside.

step 4. make the wolf and pig arms

a. With **right** sides facing and the edges aligned, machine sew each paw to each sleeve piece for the front and back pieces for all four arms. (Each paw is slightly different in shape. Make sure to carefully match up the wolf paws to the wolf sleeves and the pig paws to the pig sleeves.)

b. After all four paws are attached to the sleeve pieces, place the sleeve pieces **right** sides together with the edges aligned. Machine sew each pair together, leaving an opening at the top sleeve where the sleeve will attach to the body.

c. Stuff each paw-sleeve combo, insert in the body opening, and hand sew each arm to the body with a whipstitch and green thread.

step 5. make the wolf head

a. Using black thread, embroider two very close, vertical rows of back-stitches to make the eye slit on each white eye.

b. Using white thread and a blanket stitch, hand sew each white eye on the wolf face.

c. With the two head pieces turned with **right** sides facing and the edges aligned, pin the ears upside down and in between the head pieces.

d. Machine stitch the head pieces together, leaving the neck open.

e. Turn the head **right** side out. The ears should pop up into place.

f. Stuff the head, and stitch the neck edge closed

g. Pin the stuffed snout to the head as marked on the pattern, turning the edges under as you pin. The snout is meant to lean to the left side. To achieve that effect, turn more of the fabric under on the left side than the right, thus pulling the snout to the left.

h. Hand sew the snout to the head with brown thread and a whipstitch.

step 6. attach the wolf head to the body

a. Pin the wolf head to the body, and hand sew the two together using green thread and a whipstitch.

step 7. make the pig ears

a. Pin pink satin to the **wrong** side of each pig ear so that it will show through the V cutout in the ear. Using pink thread and working on the **right** side of the ear, machine sew the pink satin to each ear.

continued

ARTIST BIO

Lizette Greco

www.lizettegreco.com

- - - - - - - - - - - - - - -

Grew up: Chile

Creative influences: Fabric artistry runs in Lizette's family. Her tea-towel-embroidering mother, her grandmother, a professional seamstress, and her uncle, a fashion designer in her native Chile, all provided Lizette with exposure and inspiration for creating fabric arts.

Why she makes what she makes: As a mother, Lizette is inspired by her children's imaginative drawings and uses those images to develop her designs. "Making softies brings out the part of me that likes to play with things like scissors, fabrics, colors, and shapes," she says.

b. With **right** sides facing and the edges aligned, machine sew the front and back of each ear together.

c. Turn **right** side out. Set the ears aside. *Do not stuff the ears.*

step 8. make the pig snout

a. Using black thread and a backstitch, embroider a pair of oval nostrils on the front pig snout.

b. With **right** sides facing and the edges aligned, use pink thread and machine sew the top and bottom snouts together, making a long, circular strip.

c. With **right** sides facing, machine sew the front pig snout to the piece you just sewed together.

d. Turn the snout **right** side out, and set it aside.

step 9. make the pig head

a. Using black thread, embroider a French knot in the center of each white eye.

b. Using white thread and a blanket stitch, hand sew the eyes onto the pig face.

c. With **right** sides facing and the edges aligned, pin the head pieces together with the ears upside down and in between the head pieces.

d. Machine stitch the head pieces together with ears inside, leaving the neck open.

e. Turn the head **right** side out. Ears should pop up in place.

f. Pin the finished snout to the pig head, and using pink thread and a whip-stitch, hand sew the snout onto the head. Leave a 1-inch opening, and stuff the snout. Whipstitch the snout closed to finish attaching it to the head.

g. Stuff the pig head.

step 10. stuff the body, and attach the pig head

a. Stuff the body with fiberfill.

b. Pin the pig head to the body, turn the fabric under a bit, and use pink thread and a whipstitch to hand sew the two together.

wee robot

DIFFICULTY LEVEL : moderate   **FINISHED SIZE** : 4 inches wide by 4½ inches high   **SEW** : by machine and hand

This robot has a lot going for him. A good example of creative embellishment, he sports radar ears, made with doll-sized suspender clips, and a thin wire for his arms, which rotate and can be posed.

embroidery stitches

blanket stitch

whipstitch

running stitch

Note: When sewing with floss, use 6 strands unless otherwise noted.

materials

FABRIC: ¼ yard moss green wool for the body

FELT: scrap of white and a scrap of lime green for face

FLOSS: white, khaki green, beige (optional); light green

THREAD: moss green

TRIM: 2 buttons for eyes, ½ inch in diameter; 3 buttons for body decoration, ½ inch in diameter; 15-inch length 24-gauge floral paddle wire; 2 buttons for hands, ¾ inch in diameter (which should have one large center shank big enough for wire to pass through); 1 to 1½ yards of super-chunky yarn for arms; 2 suspender clips, ⅝ inch wide

OTHER: weighted filler

Note: See page 8 for the list of basic supplies needed for all projects.

cut from pattern

FROM WOOL
3 body pieces

cut freehand

FROM FELT
1 white round-edged face rectangle, 1½ by 2 inches

1 lime round-edged face rectangle, 1 by 1½ inches

FROM WOOL
1 bottom circle, 3½ inches in diameter

continued

sew

step 1. embellish the front

a. Choose one of the body pieces to be the front.

b. Using a blanket stitch and 2 strands of white floss, hand sew the white face rectangle to the body.

c. Using a blanket stitch and khaki green floss, embroider the lime upper face rectangle onto the white face.

d. Sew the button eyes on the face, and attach 3 buttons for the "control panel" at the bottom of the front piece, approximately ½ inch from the bottom edge. If you wish, add optional embroidery, sewing with beige floss above the button control panel. (A feather stitch was used for this softie, but any decorative stitch would work equally well.)

step 2. assemble the body

a. With two of the **right** sides of the body pieces facing and the edges aligned, machine stitch the pair together along the vertical seam.

b. Repeat step 2a to attach the third body piece to the other two.

c. Sew the last vertical seam, leaving 2 to 3 inches open at the back for turning the body **right** side out and stuffing it.

step 3. attach the bottom

a. With **right** sides facing and the edges aligned, pin the bottom piece to the body, making sure it fits well. Trim the bottom piece if necessary.

b. Using moss green thread, machine sew the bottom to the body, and turn the whole piece **right** side out.

step 4. stuff the robot

a. Stuff the robot three-quarters full with fiberfill. Add weighted filler at the bottom to help the robot balance.

b. Sew the opening closed by hand, using the moss green thread and a whipstitch.

continued

ARTIST BIO

Hillary Lang

WEE WONDERFULS
www.weewonderfuls.com

- - - - - - - - - - - - -

Grew up: Chicago

Creative influences: A crafty grandmother, a home economics class in high
school, and an inheritance of quilting
fabric and supplies helped launch
Hillary's crafty life.

Why she makes what she makes:
Initially inspired to make softies after
discovering Claire Robertson's Loobylu
blog (www.loobylu.com), Hillary experi-
ments with form and texture and finds
additional inspiration in Japanese
craft books.

step 5. embellish the robot

a. Hand sew a decorative running stitch on both sides of each vertical seam of the body using light green floss.

b. With the same floss, whipstitch around the bottom circle to decorate it. These whipstitches are vertical rather than slanted, but since they are for decoration only, either straight or slanted is fine.

step 6. make the arms

a. To make the arms with medium-gauge floral paddle wire, start by pok-ing the wire through the body from the left side of the robot. Push the wire through the stuffing and out the other side, keeping the wire as straight as possible so the arms will be symmetrical. The arms should be able to rotate in tandem. (If you're having trouble getting the wire through the body, thread the end of the wire onto a very long needle and pull the needle and wire through the body.)

b. Once the wire is in place, twist each wire end through a button shank for a hand.

c. Cut a 20-inch piece of super-chunky yarn, and tie a knot at one end.

d. Thread the yarn on a needle, and pull the yarn through the button hand's buttonhole three or four times to cover the wire, ending with the yarn on the upper side of the button hand.

e. Wrap the yarn around the wire arm, working up and down the arm until it has a nice, substantial thickness to it. Make sure to end wrapping the yarn at the upper arm where it attaches to the body.

f. Cut the yarn, leaving a 4-inch tail. Thread the yarn tail on an extra-long needle, and pull the tail through the center of the body and the needle out the other side, leaving the yarn tail buried inside. Pulling the yarn tail into the body helps anchor the arms.

g. Repeat steps 5c through 5f to finish the other arm.

step 7. finish the robot

a. Hand sew the suspender clips for antennae.

green cross paperweight

DIFFICULTY LEVEL : easy   **FINISHED SIZE** : 4½ wide by 4½ inches long   **SEW** : by hand

An iconic shape that lends itself well to embellishment, this paperweight features easy-to-cut felt appliqués that can be made in any shape you choose.

embroidery stitches

running stitch

whipstitch

French knot

Note: When sewing with floss, use 6 strands unless otherwise noted.

materials

FELT: scraps of peach, brown, and moss green for the appliqué decorations; 1 sheet of apple green for the front; 1 sheet of brown for the back

FLOSS: peach; moss green; brown

TRIM: 1 leaf button, ½ inch in diameter

OTHER: weighted filler

Note: See page 8 for the list of basic supplies needed for all projects.

cut from patterns

FROM FELT

1 brown cross (front)

1 green cross (back)

cut freehand

FROM FELT

peach, brown, and moss green hearts, circles, a rectangle, a crown, and flower shapes (or whatever colors and shapes you prefer)

continued

ARTIST BIO

Therese Laskey

SOFTIES CENTRAL
www.softiescentral.typepad.com

Grew up: Beirut and New York

Creative influences: Vintage trim, textile pictures, American folk art, and fashion photography from the 1950s and '60s spark Therese's creativity.

Why she makes what she makes: Fascinated and intrigued by the growing indie craft movement, Therese put this book together to showcase the breadth of imaginative designs for softies being made by the best plush artists around the world.

sew

step 1. attach appliqués to the front cross

a. Using peach floss and a running stitch, hand sew the peach and brown appliqués to the front cross, scattering the appliqués around the cross.

b. Attach a heart appliqué to the center of a rectangle with a running stitch using peach floss, and then attach the rectangle to the cross with a brown floss whipstitch.

c. Add a few French knots to the center of the flower.

d. Sew on the leaf button, and set the cross front aside.

step 2. add appliqués to the green back

a. Cut shapes like those shown in the photo or create your own.

b. Using a running stitch and matching-color floss (moss green or peach), embroider the appliqués to the back of the cross.

step 3. sew the front to the back of the cross

a. With **wrong** sides facing and edges aligned, pin the front and back cross pieces together.

b. Using brown floss, sew the pieces together with a running stitch ⅛ inch in from the edge of the fabric, leaving one side open for stuffing.

step 4. stuff and finish the cross

a. Stuff the cross with a mixture of fiberfill and weighted filler.

b. Sew the opening closed, matching the line of the running stitches.

resources

FELT AND FABRIC

A. H. MERCANTILE
fabrics including printed cottons, fleece, and oilcloth
www.ahmercantile.com

MAGIC CABIN
wool felt
www.magiccabin.com

REPRODEPOT
fabric
www.reprodepot.com

NEEDLE FELTING SUPPLIES*

MARR HAVEN
www.marrhaven.com

MIELKE'S FIBER ARTS
www.mielkesfarm.com

*You can also find foam pads at some knitting, craft, and upholstery stores.

TRIM AND OTHER CRAFT SUPPLIES

ARBEE
plastic koala bear claws
www.arbee.com.au

BJ'S CRAFT SUPPLIES
wide range of craft supplies
www.bjcraftsupplies.com

JOGGLES
beads, doll-making supplies, needle felting supplies, charms, fabric, floss, and online craft classes
www.joggles.com

M & J TRIMMING
large variety of buttons, ribbons, beads, braid, and buckles
www.mjtrim.com

TINSEL TRADING COMPANY
vintage ribbons, velvet flowers, tassels, and silver appliqués
www.tinseltrading.com

RETAIL STORES

HANCOCK FABRICS
fabric, craft felt, and sewing supplies
www.hancockfabrics.com

JO-ANN STORES
craft supplies and fabric
www.joann.com

MICHAELS
wide range of craft supplies
www.michaels.com

ONLINE TUTORIALS

AMIGURUMI TUTORIAL
www.crochetme.com/amigurumi

CRAFTSTER.ORG
www.craftster.org

WHIP UP
http://whipup.net

ONLINE SHOPS SELLING HANDMADE GOODS

You can also find handmade goods for sale on softie designers' individual blogs.

CUT + PASTE
www.cutxpaste.com

ETSY
www.etsy.com

FRED FLARE
www.fredflare.com

MAHAR DRY GOODS
www.mahardrygoods.com

MAGAZINES FOR INSPIRATION AND IDEAS

CRAFT
www.craftzine.com

MARIE CLAIRE IDÉES
www.marieclaireidees.com

READY MADE
www.readymade.com

SELVEDGE
www.selvedge.org

index

acknowledgments

Before I began researching and writing this book, I didn't realize how much I had learned about sewing from my mother. I remembered what seemed like hours drifting around the fabric store, casually looking through Butterick pattern books, fingering buttons and zippers, waiting impatiently for her to finish shopping. I remembered more time spent watching her lay fabric on the floor of her sewing room, cutting out patterns for skirts and dresses. She made a lot of my clothes, so I spent *more* time standing like a statue as she pinned and basted and tucked and snipped. Her garments were always well made—but, ungrateful child that I was, I often found fault with my homemade clothes and asked to shop from the Sears catalog instead.

I watched my crafty mother take up other pursuits—first *ikebana* (Japanese flower arranging), and then Japanese silk-flower making, followed by macramé, rug hooking, and a little left turn into leather. Throughout it all, I just read books, thoroughly engrossed in my latest library find.

Somehow, to my amazement, I found that I had absorbed some of her lessons, for as I started working with the softies in the book, tips and shortcuts came back to me, as did a love of fabric, textile, trim, and the sheer joy of making something with your hands that a minute ago was a scrap of cloth. All the lessons I had tried *not* to learn surfaced nevertheless, and so it is with deep love and honor that I thank my mother for showing me what *she* loved.

I extend many thanks also to my grandmother, who taught me to embroider and knit and introduced me to vintage pieces in her closet and chifforobe drawers. Thanks, Nana, for letting me play with your button box.

I'm grateful to Gail Harrington, an early believer in this book. I don't think I would have written the book proposal without her support and encouragement.

Thanks also are due to my agent, Lilly Ghahremani, whose advice and constructive critiques made me a better writer—and a smarter one, too. Much gratitude to everyone else at Full Circle Literary, especially Stefanie Von Borstel.

My secret weapon in the sewing world has been Cal Patch, whose advice was invaluable. I thank Chris Timmons for her pinpoint accuracy and gentle questions that sent me down the right path. I learned a lot about sewing from these two women, and I'll always be grateful to them.

Thanks to all the folks at Chronicle Books, including Jodi Warshaw and Brooke Johnson—the people who make the most beautiful craft books with care and a sense of perfection. A special shout-out goes to Kate Prouty, who has given me a great deal of priceless advice and has helped me navigate through the book-publishing process with her special brand of grace.

Finally, I'd most sincerely like to thank all my friends and family who supported me and endured months of listening to my play-by-play descriptions of softie making.

Last but also definitely *first*, my most heartfelt thanks go to the softie designers who contributed projects for the book. Thank you for trusting me with your wonderful softies. I wish the utmost success for all of you!

120